Do Not Weep

Peter N Muya

Published by Peter N Muya.

Do Not Weep

Peter N Muya

Published by Peter N Muya, 2024.

DO NOT WEEP
Peter N Muya
First edition. July 2024.
Second edition. June 2025
Copyright © 2025 Peter N Muya.
ISBN 9798227829443

For information contact Bishop Peter Muya via muyabishop@gmail.com or via phone +254724805868/+254798649468

Edited by Peter Hinga Kiago. Email: quibpet3r@gmail.com Phone +254706488565

I dedicate this book to widows and the children of the victims of drug abuse who have died prematurely leaving their families with a lot of mental torture and suffering.

It is very unfortunate that wives of the victims find themselves living desperately as widows in this hurting world. Many of them are languishing in poverty not knowing where to turn for help after losing their husbands in illicit brew consumption.

"Fear Not, Only Believe. Do Not Weep"
Bishop Peter N Muya.

Foreword

"PURE AND GENUINE RELIGION in the sight of God the Father means caring for orphans and widows in their distress and refusing to let the world corrupt you" (James 1:27). Peter Muya's classic book *Do Not Weep* explains and defines with great clarity the numerous problems facing Kenya today, but also in the entire continent of Africa. The topics Peter covers includes:

As an accomplished author myself, I have written six books with one of them accepted in the esteemed United States Library of Congress. Therefore, I know a good book and a good author, and Peter and his book are great examples. The way Peter writes this book will keep you focused as to plight of the major issues. Peter shows great skill in how he puts the topics together and how they flow as one cohesive thought process.

The book informs the readers that we are not to "weep" but rejoice in the fact that God is raising up many workers who will put their hand to the plow and share the love of Jesus Christ. Many places throughout Scripture exhort people to not ignore street kids, widows and orphans. There are even warnings against mistreating these people as we read in Exodus 22:22–24, "You must not afflict any widow or orphan.

If you afflict them in any way and they cry to me, I will surely hear their cry, and my anger will burn and I will kill you with the sword, and your wives will be widows and your children will be fatherless." Therefore, we should intercede through fervent prayer for all of these situations. The situation is complicated, and we need the mind of God as the solutions.

I can personally identify with the issues described in the book. In my location where I live in the United States we have a very bad homeless problem. Many of these homeless people are orphaned adults. Issues associated with the tribal fighting are actually an opportunity to reach people for the gospel. I hear the spirit of God speaking to my heart that it is now time for the church to "penetrate the darkness."

In the body of the Book, Peter describes how the church needs to reach people who are involved in violent acts between tribes. You will also read about how corrupt politicians hinder efforts. Peter brings up the point about "widows who are widows indeed." Unfortunately, there are people who try to take advantage of programs designed to help both orphans and widows. We need to also seek the mind of God as is written in Romans 8:26–27, "Likewise the Spirit also helps in our weaknesses. For we do not know what we should pray for as we ought, but the Spirit Himself makes intercession for us with groaning's which cannot be uttered.

Now He who searches the hearts knows what the mind of the Spirit is, because He makes intercession for the saints according to the will of God." Also, in this manner we should do as Paul says in 1 Corinthians 14:1, "Pursue love and earnestly desire the spiritual gifts especially that you might prophesy." Yet in 1 Corinthians 12:31 Paul tells us to seek after the "greater gifts." Paul does not explain in this epistle what the greater gifts are, but they are working of miracles and gifts of healings. In the book Peter writes about the following points which I want to confirm in the Holy Spirit that Peter has an ear the hear the Lord,

"We are obeying the Word, which says, "Learn to do good, relieve the oppressed, defend the fatherless and plead for the widows" (Isaiah 1:17). We must be moved by compassion, which will make us break all cultural barriers as we move through the streets, slums, and ghettos to rescue these hurting souls. Just for a moment, try to put yourself in these kids' shoes. I know you will do something about them. Let's lead these widows to sustainable development before it is too late. We must have counseling programs for these widows."

Those called to walk with Peter at this moment in relation to this book should contact Peter in how they can help. Let those of us in the army of the Lord come together in unity.

By Apostle **GEORGE GATES JR**
{APOSTOLIC AND PROPHETIC MINISTRY USA}

Acknowledgement

I WANT TO THANK ARCH Bishop Dr. Arthur Gitonga of Redeemed Gospel Church a very powerful preacher of the word of God. After working under him for more than 10 years, I saw my church experiencing phenomenal growth.I started practicing his teachings of expressing practical love to the physical needs of the hopeless and the hurting. Through his bible based messages, I received what I call a wake up call to go out and do what I was called to do, ministering to desperate street kids and widows. Let me thank the leaders of Stay Up Rehabilitative Community Based Organization for giving me moral support.

Also, may I thank my editor and proofreader Peter Hinga for his excellent work.

Introduction

WHEN GOD GAVE ME A vision of giving hope to the hopeless, I started searching scriptures focusing on the widows and the hurting, God called me to rescue them from evil behaviors and hopelessness. Many of them have drowned into the sea of fear of the unknown and stress. It's only the biblical message that can help them to create a spiritual relationship with God our creator who is able to bless them physically, mentally and spiritually. As the author I'm making the glory of God to shine in the hearts of widows today.

I do believe that the word of God in this book is compelling, convincing, encouraging and most importantly redeeming the hopeless widows from hopelessness and poverty. I tried to weave together profound biblical reflections from the gospel doctrine that can change their lives and make them useful people in the community.

This book is a must read to the widows who are willing to know the truth about deliverance from stress, hopelessness and poverty. I have seen many victims of circumstances and widows being delivered by accepting that they are lost and that they need help

Read this book and join me in helping this crooked generation to confess their sins and receive Jesus Christ as their savior. Many widows will be delivered and transformed after reading and acting upon the word of God.

This is a very powerful memoir in a series of inspiring hope. The book explains the word of God in depth to the widows and I purposely address their spiritual, physical and financial problems. Do you want to be set free from the cares of this dying and hurting world? Read this book and your life will not be the same again My message to you, " Do Not Weep! Weeping may endure for a night, but joy comes in the morning". {Psalms.30. 5..}

BISHOP PETER N MUYA

CHAPTER ONE

FEAR NOT, ONLY BELIEVE

I SAT BESIDE THE FIREPLACE opposite to my family deeply considering my spiritual condition in the sight of God. — "-Fear not, only believe"{ Mark 5.36] When I read this inspiring scriptures,.I was both relaxed and excited by a wonderful and thrilling revelation of Gods word that came to my mind. I looked at my bible again. What a lovely piece of truth! I thought of the days of my past life in Jesus.

I felt proud, too, because within every page in the bible, I could find everything to satisfy my longing, and with no doubt I believed that the Bible was the Word of God; full of wonderful promises that were so appealing to me.In the year 1984 my father died and my mother became a widow. My sister died in the year 2000, my brother followed in the year 2003 and my mother in the year 2015.

I rededicated my life to serving God more than before. This was a life of resilience. As a human being these deaths of my loved ones brought a flood of emotions and a sense of uncertainty, but as a servant of GOD I encouraged myself in the Lord. A song flashed in my mind, "When peace, like a river, comes my way, when sorrows like sea billows roll; whatever my lot, you have taught me to say, Its well, It's well, with my soul."

My heart throbbed faster as I remembered the night when Jesus peered into my soul and made me a completely new person. I shall never forget that feeling that came inside of me. I was overwhelmed by emotions as the past memories came to my mind and I thought, *I am free from worry anxiety, fear, resentment, bitterness, hatred, shame, feelings of inferiority, and withdrawal.*

Before I received Jesus as my personal savior, my life had no meaning. It was miserable, empty, confused, and frustrated. I had no hope. But now, with Jesus at the center of it, there is an inner strength, a sense of peace, a deep satisfaction, and an unfading joy in my life. that's why God called me so that I can be able to encourage the widows. I teach them how to adapt well to life-changing and stressful situations. This is resilience and it is an ongoing process that requires time and effort.

By receiving Jesus Christ as my personal Savior, I was born again. It required no effort of mine that I may obtain this spiritual blessing; because I believed, it happened. Praise His wonderful name: Jesus! "I prevented the dawning of the morning and cried. I hope in thy word" *(Psalms 119:147). I teach widows the importance hoping and trusting in the lord, this involves behavior, thoughts and actions that every widow should learn and develop. We are called to seek the kingdom of God first and other things will follow us*

By faith, in Jesus Christ we were given power to become Sons of God who once were very far from religious observations and nurtured false hopes. False hopes are increasing in the world today; yet, many exist among many as to where the spiritual blessings can be found. Let me say that even though beautiful and impressive religious cathedrals are constructed, men and women are still longing for the blessing that is promised by the true word of God. In the Bible we read, "Remember the word unto thy servant, upon which thou hast caused me to hope" *(Psalms 119:49)*.

You may say, "I read the Bible daily in my life." However, does reading the Bible daily make you a Christian? No! Jesus said, "Verily, verily, I say unto thee, unless a man be born again, he cannot see the Kingdom of God" *(John 3:3)*.

DO NOT WEEP

Are you a born-again believer in Jesus Christ? Are your sins forgiven through His cleansing blood? The truth is if have no an inward witness of the Spirit in the word of salvation, you cannot be a member of Christ's church on Earth. A member of the divine family is among the holy angels and all blood-washed saints from every nation and every age. So, don't assume that simply attending religious services or reading the Bible makes you a Christian. No! Unless the power of the living God does something in you, you will perish in Hell.

Many people today lay their hope of salvation on such things as sacraments, pilgrimages, burning candles, priests, etc. But I always ask, "Did Jesus teach any such doctrine of dead traditions?" Surely not! For there is no sect, bishop, priest, ordinance, nor sacrament on Earth that can save your sinful life or give you inward peace, love, and joy. You may blindly join in to the best sect in the world and be most faithful to its doctrines and yet still be lost in Hell forever, so what is the use? I teach widows how to receive Jesus in their lives so that they can attract God's blessings in their lives. I teach them how to set realistic goals and work towards achieving them. I encourage them to depend confidently on God rather than depending on relatives.

I have the witness of God's power in my life because I am a born-again believer and I know by faith that my name is written in the Book of Life. I also have received the infilling of the Holy Spirit and do speak in tongues. The Spirit has also forged a bond between Jesus and His body, which is of the holy, blood-washed saints worldwide. I also have fellowship with brethren, which means to share the word of God with other believers in a local assembly. The word of God says, "Not forsaking the assembling of ourselves together as the manner of some is, but exhorting one another and so much more as you see the day approaching" *(Heb. 10:25).*

I did not let my relatives push me into their own religion, and I was not impressed by their nice ministers nor their big cathedrals. What I did trust on was the Lord, Jesus Christ, who gave a clear pattern of worship in the Book of Acts. It is obvious that by much prayer and Bible study, I understood God's will. God is ever faithful if our eyes of faith are fixed on Him only. He works miracles. By faith, he led Moses and the people of God. He gave them a clear pattern of worship. He said, "Who serve unto the example and shadow of heavenly things, as Moses was admonished of God when he was about to make the tabernacle: for, see, saith He, who thou make all things according to the pattern showed to thee in the mount" *(Heb. 8:5).*

The building you worship in, whether it be at home, a hall, a big cathedral, etc., has no spiritual significance whatsoever. Read the Bible well and you will find that it is the worshipers who are the Church, not the building. Therefore, you must not allow any superstitious awe of buildings or sect dignitary or Hollywood-style liturgy to dominate your thinking or make you decide your choice of fellowship. Remember that "Howbeit the Most High dwells not in the temples made with hands, as saith the prophet" *(Act 7:48).* You had better receive Jesus as your savior now by obeying God's word and straight away promising to commit yourself to obedience to God's word in every department of your life; do that, and you will be a son of God.

As a disciple of Jesus Christ, I do not lead myself. I will never allow any sect dignitary to assume God's authority. He is my Lord, and only in Him will I give account; without the false advocacy of a priest or minister. When I finally settled in my fellowship, I was able to say before them that "God has led me into this fellowship." I was separated from this sinful world and its ways and its companionship.

I could no longer attend movies or disco halls, for I was a new creature. God forbids this in His word: "Therefore, if any man be in Christ, he is a new creature and old things are passed away. Behold, all things have become new" *(II Corinthians 5:17)*. Therefore, I have to obey the Word. I encourage the widows to never quit no matter what, they should not allow life's circumstances to push them down, but they should learn to overcome by faith in Christ.

Be strong in the lord and let the storm pass without breaking your heart. Waiting upon the lord this day's demands spiritual resilience. This is the secret of survival. The more you believe in God, the you will survive. Learn to live with other believers in peace and God will bless you.

In my fellowship with other believers, God was present in the Holy Spirit, and I recognized His presence when the Word quickened my spirit, stimulated my faith, and drew out a strong desire to tell others of this wonderful experience. After my salvation, my old habits "passed away," and I became an avid reader of Christian books by anointed men of God. I received power and grew in the word of faith. Therefore, brought upon me was a consuming desire to preach the gospel, and finally I had surrendered my life to the ministry.

So, if you are not born again, you cannot be a member of the holy spiritual church that Jesus founded. The word "church" translated from the Greek, simply meaning "a called-out gathering of born-again believers." Those people who have separated themselves from the world to serve God through Jesus, His son. The Church is not a building as you tend to think. It is a sure sign that you are really born – by the power of the Spirit of God and when your soul thirsts for the truth and your heart is drawn to other believers with a desire to learn more of Jesus Christ from His word.

Is this how you are? As in that you must not want to be saved unless you feel that you are lost in sin, just as you would not plead to be rescued unless you were really drowning. Or that you would never call for a doctor unless you are sick, and just the same, you would never call for Jesus to save you unless you felt that you were a lost sinner. The Bible says, "For whosoever shall call upon the name of the Lord shall be saved" *(Romans 10:13).*

Beware of any hope that is not drawn from the Bible, for such hope is false hope. Jesus alone is the sure foundation of a Good Hope. He is the tried chief corner stone. "Wherefore also it is contained in the Scriptures... Behold. I lay in Zion a chief cornerstone elected and precious, and he who believe of Him shall not be confounded" *(1 Peter 2:6). Believing in GOD will kick out your fears, anxiety worry, hopelessness and shame. By resilience I'm able to focus on my ministry of encouraging widows, dubbed, Do Not Weep.*

Lord Thou Art My Hope
Lord I do trust in thee from my youth
Upon thee I have learned after the new birth
Thou art thee who saved me from Hell
Lord thou art my hope.
I have been a laughing stock to my friends
But Lord thou art my strong refuge
My mouth is filled with thy praise
And thy glory all the day long
Do not cast me off from thee for

DO NOT WEEP

Lord thou art my hope.
Lord make haste to help me
Let them fail whom seek my life
Rescue me, O' Lord, from the wicked generation
Be quick to deliver me
For in the Lord do I take refuge
Lord thou art my hope.
Thou art my hope and my salvation
While my enemies are against me
Let them be confused whom seek my life
And I will hope thee continually
And praise thee more and more
Lord thou art my hope.
Lord thou has crushed the oppressor
And thou has given me eternal life
My lips will shout for joy and sing praises
Dear Lord thou art good to me
May thy Name be praised forever for
Lord thou art my hope.

In my ministry as a pastoral councilor, I have learnt four sets of outstanding mental attitude which becomes a threat in the lives of believers and especially widows. Let me group these sets as follows:

1. Fear, anxiety and worry
2. Resentment, bitterness and hatred
3. Shame, feelings of inferiority and withdrawal
4. Hopelessness, guilt and self- destruction.

I have gained more advice from psychiatrist and psychologists regarding these common issues that are affecting many people in the society especially widows. Many widows are suffering silently without knowing which way to turn for help. By faith in Jesus Christ there is assurance of healing and deliverance from these hurting issues.

I am helping many to overcome these problems although some are wondering whether the word of God has something to offer by way of healing or deliverance. . with God nothing is impossible. The truth Is in the word of God there is healing and deliverance from all problems affecting any human being in this hurting world.

1.Fear, anxiety and worry

WHEN MY MOTHER DIED, God gave me a burden to minister hope to the hopeless and encourage the widows. I started a ministry to help them escape from hopelessness, worry, anxiety, fear, resentment, bitterness, hatred, shame, feeling of inferiority, withdrawal, guilt and self- destruction.

I tell widows that it is unwise to continue harboring this evil thing in their hearts without doing something to erase them. In the bible Jesus encouraged one widow who was weeping because her only son had died "Do not weep" Luke 7:13. The bible in Isaiah 54:4 says " fear not for you will not be ashamed the reproach of your widow-hood, you will remember no more. Verse 5 says," for your maker is your husband"

To the ruler of a synagogue Jesus encouraged him because his daughter had died" fear not, only believe" (mark 5 -36). I emulate Jesus Christ in my ministry that's why I encourage widows using the word of God- the key word to widows, "Do not weep" the second word is" fear not, only believe"

DO NOT WEEP

The motto of the ministry to the widows is "Do not weep" do not let this conditions or evil habits control your life, because this can lead you to self- harm. Do not destroy yourself by committing suicide.

Many widows are suffering from these three things, but mostly they are suffering from worry without knowing. This behavior has brought many widows to a state of tension which causes chronic fatigue in their bodies. Victims start by complaining of feeling very tired all the time.

I help the victims by telling them to download worries out of their minds because it explodes into depression and leads to other mental sicknesses. Download your mind by talking to your pastor or a trained counselor. Some widows are brought in my office suffering from these things with nervousness and emotional tensions. I counsel them and pray with them and they are healed or delivered in Jesus name.

In my ministry to the widows, I can confidently say that faith works. Do not doubt, take a step of faith and seek help. These problems can cause mental sickness in your life. Come and let us reason together, fear not only believe.

These things will load your mind with indecision, vague wishes, procrastination, unsolved troubles, grudges, jealousy and dissatisfaction. These could cause nervous and emotional tensions. Clean off your mind from time to time by talking to your pastor or your counselor.

Jesus commanded us not to worry – "Do not worry, saying what shall we eat? Or what shall we drink? Or what shall we wear?" (Mathew 6: 31) You should not worry because verse 34 says "Do not worry about tomorrow" in James 4:13-14 we are warned not to say "today or tomorrow we will go to such and such a city, spend a year there, buy and sell and make profit whereas you do not know what happens tomorrow".

Jesus has given us the reason of not to worry – 'For your heavenly father knows that you need all these things' (Mathew 6:32) The answer to everybody and mostly to the widows who live with self- pity and low self- esteem', Do not worry because your heavenly father knows all these problems you are facing now. So relax and trust in Him. But if you haven't surrendered your life to Him you will worry.

I don't want to waste my time to encourage anybody suffering from these things with empty words; 'do not worry' this words cannot heal you without trusting in the word of God. Jesus Christ has power to save you from your sins and heal you from fear, worry, anxiety etc.

Jesus has given us the solution in (Mathew 6:33) "Seek ye first the kingdom of God and His righteousness and all these things shall be added unto you". Start your journey by surrendering your life to God, receive His kingdom and let other things follow you. God knows all our needs and He is the source of our supply.

When a baby cries in discomfort and it gets soothing words from the mother, the mother gives the baby attention, care and satisfaction. Since God has become our father by receiving his kingdom, we have no need to worry or fear. Learn to say that "If the lord wills, we shall do this or that" (James 4:15).

Apostle Peter taught us 'Cast all your cares upon Him, for He cares for you' cast all your cares to God for He cares for you. Do not cast your cares to anybody else in this world. Not even your husband, wife, mum, father, brother, sister, friend or relatives. You will be cursed because of trusting in human beings- 'Cursed is the man who trusts in man and makes flesh his strength" (Jeremiah

17:5) by living by faith and trusting in God you will be blessed. Blessed is the man who trusts in the Lord, trust is in the lord" (Jeremiah 17:7).

2. Resentment, bitterness, hatred

WHEN YOU ALLOW RESENTMENT to grow in your heart it turns to bitterness and later becomes hatred. the victim will notice that every part of the body is stirred up and prepared for action. The victim might cause physical violence or verbal abuse. Because of anger, certain parts of the body could stir action. Therefore, we should not harbor or entertain resentment, bitterness or hatred in our hearts, it will destroy us. Do not hate people physically or mentally. The bible warns us' Better is a dinner of herbs where love is than a fatted calf with hatred" (proverbs 17:1) Leviticus law is written," You shall not hate your brother in your heart" (Leviticus 19:17). Jesus taught about, hatred' But I say to you, love your enemies, bless those who curse you, do good to those who hate you, and pray for those who spiritually use you and' persecute you' (Mathew 5:44). Let's open our hearts to God by avoiding resentment, bitterness and hatred. That will give us inner peace and inexpressible joy.

3. Shame, Inferiority and Withdrawal

MANY A TIMES WE HAVE felt something that has made us hurt, slightly left out, ignored or make us feel not worth, self-esteem or rejected. Hurt feelings are very dangerous because an injured heart could make you feel ashamed with a sense of inferiority. It is natural to protect your -self from shame because it can cause you to withdraw from your social contacts for feeling inferior. Never try to hide your feelings of inferiority because it could lead you to withdraw from reality. You can get into very harmful feeling of hopelessness.

Never compare yourself with others because you are original. The cure for inferiority, shame and withdraw is humility. The bible says – 'God resists the proud but gives grace to the humble" (James 4:6) Jesus said – 'Whoever exalts himself will be humbled". When pride comes, then shame follows' pride brings shame" (proverbs 11:2)

Humility rules out hidden inferiority feelings. In humility there is no pride.

4 Guilt, Hopelessness and Self –Harm

THE FEELING OF GUILT and hopelessness started with Adam and Eve in the garden of Eden when they sinned. When any child disobeys his/her parents they suffer from guilt. Guilt feelings start in our conscience judging us because of our wrong doings. Repentance of sins makes the blood of Jesus to cleanse our guilty conscience and we receive inner peace together with joy. Feelings of guilt are as old as mankind. Cain killed his brother Abel and he suffered for his guilt.

Mankind has suffered from the beginning because of guilt. Guilt is a feeling for having done wrong. it's a judging mental attitude. Guilt is a curse because it is caused by disobedience. there are promises of blessings to all those who obey God like Abraham. In the book of Deuteronomy 28:1-14 We have a record of all the blessings and all the curses start from the15th verse, but let me quote verse 65-67 '' The lord will give you a trembling heart and failing eyes, anguish of soul, your life shall hang in doubt before you, and you shall fear day and night and have no assurance of life. In the morning you shall say' oh' that it was evening and in the evening you shall say 'oh' that it was morning, because of the fear that terrifies your heart and because of the sight which your eyes see" (Duet 28:65-67).

This verse has the true picture of guilt feelings and fear. Fear, guilt and hopelessness are curses which can lead to self- harm like suicide. The feelings of guilt can cause you to feel that no one cares for you or loves you. It removes your hope of living so the devil gives you an option to go and commit suicide. 'anyone who commits suicide goes straight to hell.

The best thing to remove guilt is to repent your sins and call the name of Jesus to save you from sins. Don't rely on your strength and never compare yourself with others. You are God's best. The only solution for overcoming all these dangers in your life is to trust in God your maker. He has power to forgive you and help you live by faith in his word. There is everything to help you in this world and you can be blessed spiritually, physically and mentally. God loves you.

The first thing that will make God to bless you is to seek his kingdom first and his righteousness and other things will be added to you. (Mat 6:33). How do you seek the kingdom of God? is by repenting your sins and receiving Jesus Christ as your personal savior. These are the things that could bring healing, deliverance, infilling of the Holy Spirit and financial blessings in your life.

You should be faithful in giving God tithes and offerings. Obedience and faithfulness can trigger God's overflowing blessings in your life. " Bring the full tithe into my storehouse, that there may be food in my house, and thereby put me into test, says the

Lord of host. And see if I will not open the windows of heaven for you and pour down for you a blessing until there is no more need '' (malachi:3-10) verse 8 ''Will man rob God? Yet you are robbing me.

Do not rob God and expect him to bless you. Many people are suffering in fear, worry, anxiety, resentment, hatred, bitterness, feeling inferior, guilt and hopelessness because of ignorance and disobedience. People are living in stress, depression and mental sickness because they don't want to obey the word of God. Are you obeying or disobeying the word of God? Let me encourage you – "Weep no more, behold the lion of the tribe of Judah, the root of David has conquered. (Rev 5:5) who is the lion of the tribe of Judah who has conquered? Jesus Christ the son of the living God. Weeping may endure for a night, but joy comes in the morning" (psalm 30:5) your joy has come.

Healing from Fear, Anxiety and Worry.

AS A PASTOR GOD HAS given me a burden to encourage widows. Are you a widow who is suffering in any way? If you are suffering, the future can look grey and miserable. Eternity is a terrifying word to think of when one feels she is standing on its brink. Do you know that God in His infinite love has permitted you to come to this extremity so that He might make Himself known to you? It is only when human beings get into hopeless situations that they are open to listening to God's voice.

From my own experience, I can assure any widow that out of your present distress, our God can bring you the greatest blessing you have ever known. Please, believe this. The Bible says, "And all things whatsoever ye shall ask for in prayer, believing ye shall receive" *(Matthew 21:22)*.

DO NOT WEEP

Jesus is inviting you to ask for your salvation and your healing from fear, anxiety and worry now. If you could only believe, His hand is stretched out to touch you at this very moment. All you need to do is receive Him by faith. He cannot work without your cooperation. He cannot give you the gift of salvation or inner peace until you put your faith into action.

For Healing from resentment, bitterness and hatred, this is what the scripture means: "But without faith, it is impossible to please Him" *(Heb. 11:6)*. When in prayer, believe that God has heard your prayer the first time you pray because God does not need to be coaxed to answer prayers. It is important that you understand this; otherwise, you will pray in vain repetitions and get nothing in the end. God hears prayers the first time you pray in earnest. After pray you can boldly confess that, thank you God for hearing my prayers for now I'm free from the spirit of resentment, bitterness and hatred.

Jesus is saying to you now: "Who forgives all thine iniquities; who heals all thine diseases" *(Psalms 103:3)*. Jesus expects you to respond in faith saying, "Thank you, Lord. I take you at your word and believe that you have forgiven me now." It is not praying that makes you obtain, but rather believing is receiving.

Hear what Jesus said before raising a man from the dead: "Said I not unto thee, that if thou would believe, thou should see the glory of God" *(John 11:40)*. Many widows today like hearing about God, but they do not want to believe in Him; hence, they can't see the glory of God (Job 42:5). I teach widows how they can be delivered from the spirit of shame, feelings of inferiority and withdrawal. After prayer praise GOD for answering your prayers.

Believing must always come before seeing or feeling, so do not be surprised if you feel a little change after receiving salvation or healing. Jesus comes in very softly. It is almost certain that Satan tries to resist the fullness of salvation or healing in order to try your faith.

Never let down God's promises when you pray. Never doubt that God has saved you or healed you when you believed. Keep on thanking and praising Jesus, for He is still working in your life. He will not fail you no matter how helpless your case is. Be content to praise and to stand by God's words. Believe God that He is going to deliver you from the spirit of hopelessness, guilt and self-destruction. Thank Him for answering your prayers and move on by faith.

We have a good instance of this in the cleansing of the lepers. Having accepted Jesus's word, "They walked on in trust, and as they went, they were cleansed" *(Luke 17:14)*. Immediately they believed the healing process had started, and it became fully manifested in their bodies. We have a similar instance in John 4:50, where the healing power of Christ was immediately set in motion when the nobleman accepted His word in faith. If you believe His saving power is working in you, then confess your faith to someone, as commanded by God in Romans 10:9-10. Simply say, "Jesus Christ is saving me now," and point to the Word as proof. Others may start to believe, too. There is nothing that is more faith-strengthening than a bold confession from your mouth. Read II Corinthians 4:13. I encourage every widow to speak what she believes in the word of GOD, is very powerful.

What is your scriptural authority for expecting God to your answer prayers at the first time? It is found in Mark 11:24. "What things so ever you ask for, when you pray, believe you receive and ye shall have them." Note that the Lord did not say that I was to receive in the future. Rather, it said, "Believe you receive." This simply means that whatever needs you have, God will meet them at this minute, if you believe you receive. Believing is the condition of receiving. Ever since I learned to exercise this faith, I have never remained the same. It is like plugging into divine power while praises keep the power flowing. Praise Works Wonders.

For every burden you have and every need you have, you normally commit it to God in definite faith, whether it be healing, sanctification, or power for service or deliverance from hopelessness or stress. You believe God gives, and you are freed from the burden and freed from the miserable bondage of repetitive praying that so wearies the soul and destroys faith. Learn to wait upon God, suppose it takes time to obtain the blessings. You keep on praising God for reminding your heart of my faith transaction and God's faithfulness (Romans 4:18-25). Once you learn this way of praising, you will know a new way of living and see quicker answers to your prayers, especially in your own life in matters of sanctification your, needs or spiritual power. Praise performs wonders; somehow, prayers cannot.

Whenever you thank God, even if you are in times of severe tests of faith, you will find the spirit of God flooding your soul in a wonderful way. Let me tell you that it is not easy to praise God when you are in pain or weakness or when you are brokenhearted. It is not easy to praise God when everything seems opposite. However, I can assure you from my own experience that praise is the sure way of victory. (Read Acts 16:25-26; 2nd Chron : 20:20).

No matter how hopeless the situation, no matter how hardhearted the person we are praying for is, the praise of faith works wonders. Praise hooks the fish; praise lands it on shore. What a difference it makes in my life when I wake up in the morning with thanks and praise on my lips for the wonders God did for me the previous day and for the marvelous things He is going to do today and every day; till I see His face.

A life filled with such praise is a holy, God-pleasing life. The law of faith applies to the vilest sinner who honestly wants to seek God. Apart from this faith, there is no widow who will ever receive pardon nor experience the saving power of Jesus Christ. Faith is the key to every blessing. Widows who are enjoying secret sins or who hold grudges need not offer this prayer of faith. God does not hear hypocrites unless they repent. I want every widow to declare with me.

"Behold. Jesus Christ is my salvation. I will trust and not be afraid, for the Lord Jehovah is my strength and song. He also became my salvation" *(Isaiah 12:2)*. He is your savior when you so claim Him. It is not a question of feeling saved or healed. It is a question of taking God at His word. Faith Is Not Feelings. It cannot be emphasized enough that in any faith transaction, we must absolutely disregard your feelings. What you feel and what you see are very often Satan's weapons to make you disbelieve God's word. What God says is fact to faith. (Read Heb. 11:1, II Cor. 4: As a widow God loves you and the bible says He is your husband so trust in Him by walking by faith and not by sight.

What is your need at this moment? Jesus is speaking to you now, saying, have faith in God (Mark 11:22) and then speak to your mountain (Mark 11:23). Command your mountain to leave in Jesus's name! Jesus Christ can break every sin and disease that Satan has brought to you. The Lord is saying, "I am the Lord who health thee" *(Exodus 15:26)*. Why not believe He is SPEAKING TO YOU and promising to deliver you? Take by faith His saving and healing power.

Say to Him now, "Jesus, will you come into my life in saving power and completely deliver me from evil?" As a widow, if you refuse Jesus Christ, what other hope can you have? Believe now and receive now (Matthew 21:22). Speak to your problem and command it to leave in Jesus's name. God bless you. This is a voice of encouragement to all widows in this hurting world.

CHAPTER TWO

DO NOT WEEP

LUCY WANJIRU IS A COMMITTED Christian in the Kiambogo Village, Gilgil District Nakuru County. She had gone to visit her relatives in Gwakiongo Centre near Nyahururu. Unfortunately, on her way home, tragedy hit near Kunste Hotel, just a few kilometers from Nakuru Town.

The Matatu she was travelling in was involved in a fatal accident. Lucy heard a loud bang. She later learned that passerby had not expected any survivors from the wrecked vehicle and therefore they evacuated passengers from the back. Many people died on the spot, but Lucy survived death by a whisker. Survivors, including her, were rushed to the Provincial General Hospital in Nakuru Town. Doctors immediately amputated a badly crushed leg. This was a terrible day for Lucy, a kind of baptism by fire.

A friend informed her husband, George, and their children. Their anxiety heightened when the gatekeepers at the hospital would not allow them in until 1:00 pm. After what seemed like an eternity to Lucy's family, the gatekeepers allowed them in. Surprisingly, her husband seemed to be calm and strong in the Lord because he was a committed Christian, along with his wife. He consoled his overwhelmed and emotional children. He was telling them to accept God's will on their mother's life. George led his children in thanking God that his wife's life was saved from death, even though her one leg was missing.

"What happened?" was the first question that Lucy asked people in the hospital when she regained consciousness. She was told that her life was in danger and that nobody knew if she was going to survive. Lucy had multiple fractures, and her body was aching. Her hair thinned out, and sores covered many parts of her body. She could only be fed intravenously and could not communicate coherently. She battled with the deteriorating condition as the hospital bill soared.

God is good. After months in the hospital, her condition improved. She was put on medications and special diets before being discharged from the hospital, praise God! At home, Lucy had to rely on other people to do even the simplest errands. She has been asking well-wishers, individuals, and organizations like, Stay Up Rehabilitative Community Based Organization to help her get an artificial leg, as well as money for her family's upkeep. Her husband is jobless and has nothing to provide for her.

Some years, Lucy was living with her daughter in Lanet so she could make regular visits to the hospital. God is good for providing her with a plot and a house where she is living with her husband George., She continues with physiotherapy and visits the orthopedic rehabilitation center. She also continues with her counseling sessions at the hospital.

Today, she has adjusted minimally to her new status, and she is doing all she can to continue living positively by the grace of God. Lucy is going to prove to the world that disability is not inability. With God, everything is possible. She intends to start a dress-making course, and she is also learning business skills.

Lucy wants to start sharing her living testimony with the world in her vision, known as "A Survivors Vision" Please support this vision. Losing one leg in a road crash is unbearable, but Lucy is thanking God for giving her a chance to survive. She is asking you to help her weave her life back together. God bless you. Thank you.

DO NOT WEEP

As a full-time pastor, God called upon me to give hope to the hopeless and encourage the hurting. When Lucy Wanjiru Karanja was involved in a near-death accident and survived by God's grace alone, I went to her home to encourage her and her husband.

I quoted the Scriptures from Luke chapter seven, verse thirteen, "Do not weep." Lucy was strengthened, and she opened up. She shared with me her vision of helping orphans and vulnerable children. She told me how their family members decided to raise money to buy her an artificial leg and pay her hospital bill.

I listened to her as she told me that the chairman who was chosen to lead the committee did not take his responsibilities seriously, and he did not show up in the meetings. For reasons I could not control or understand, I secretly started finding ways to raise money to support this needy family. Lucy's legal advocate tried to fight in the courts for her compensation, but the court delayed her case. She is hopeless.

I said in my heart that I was going to make the world know about Lucy's case and donate something to her. That's why I'm writing Lucy's story so that you give in support for her physical needs. I'm planning to print proforma posters and arrange quests to attend this important fundraising event.

Before I invited ministers, artists, choirs, and politicians to help this needy family While we were waiting for this event, the WORLD VISION through their office Kiambogo; in Eburu ward, Gilgil subcounty, Nakuru, donated a wheelchair for Lucy. Thank God for their love and generosity in support of Lucy; Anther institution in Nairobi helped her get funding for an artificial leg. God is moving mightily in Lucy's life. Despite her disability, God has helped her to encourage kids who are hurting. She is a motivational speaker to the hopeless. She is proving to the world that her disability is not inability. Without a leg but with God, she can encourage millions through her written and spoken messages. She has very inspiring and encouraging messages. Read her story on the Internet.

It is estimated that there are millions of hopeless people like widows or orphans left by those who die of HIV/AIDS pandemics and other common problems in Africa. Our ministry is teaching our members their role in assisting the widows in their affliction. We advise them to form small community-based originations (C.B.O.). We ask them to participate fully in secular models of social work, which can help them earn some money to meet their needs.

To us, love is not just defined as a wonderful feeling in our hearts, but also to act lovingly to help the needy widows in this life. The Bible says the blessing of him that was ready to perish came upon me: "...and I caused the widows heart to sing for joy" (Job 29:13).

God has given us a burden in ministering to the widows we are helping, even those who are suffering from different kinds of problems with somebody else to assist them. We are called to show God's love in action. The Bible says that true love seecatch not her own; it does not behave rudely. Love is not easily provoked; it thinks no evil. Love does not force someone to give or to do good to anybody. Love makes us focus on helping the needy widows.

Love does not make someone puffed up or proud. Love makes us humble and kind to others. Love makes us share some of our resources with the less fortunate. It's our prayer that God will open your eyes to see the need to help the widows around you. Find your area of ministry to widows. Join us in making a difference in this hurting world. Remember that the mission field is close to your home.

Just like the Good Samaritan in the Bible, who shows love and mercy to the one who was severely injured by the enemy, be a channel of God's flowing blessings to others, and you will receive an overflowing blessing in return. Real love makes you take action to help others in need. The Bible says, "And whatever you do, do it heartily as to the Lord, knowing that from the Lord you will receive the reward" (Col. 3:23,24).

We are doing everything to improve the lives of the widows. Remember. Everything you give to anyone in need, including a cup of cold water, has eternal value when you do it in Jesus' name.

All that you do to others will be done to you in return. And one day before meeting the King of Kings, you will be given your reward for your good work. Let's show the highest kind of love from the depth of our hearts to the widows. Jesus Christ is willing to meet all the needs of the widows. We are encouraging them to make God their only hope. God is their brightest hope and is more than an ordinary husband. We advise them to preach the gospel to others and trust God to meet their needs. The Bible says, "for thy maker is thine husband" (Isa. 54:5).

Are you a widow? God is your husband. Tell him all of your needs. If you have problems you would like to discuss with us, call or write to our office. We are ready to help you. God bless you! A "widow" is any woman who has lost her husband by death. After the burial of her husband, and after a period of mourning, the widow may experience problems from her husband's relatives because of the traditions and cultures of different tribes in our society.

Some men in the family would want to marry the widow against her will, and others would want all of the possessions of her husband, leaving her with nothing. We have young widows and old widows. For young widows, the Bible releases them to get married again. Older widows can remain widows and serve God in the church for the rest of their lives.

We encourage them through our outreach program. Instead of weeping, they are encouraged to start income-generating projects, and many are doing very well in small businesses. I encourage them by reading the story of Naomi, a widow, and Ruth, her daughter-in-law (Ruth 1:1-21).

The deepest inner pain is that no one can explain how it feels to lose someone you love. Many widows are suffering both mentally and physically. Only the widow who knows the pain of widowhood, and only the orphan who knows the pain of being an orphan, is ready to hear from us.

We minister hope to all those widows who are suffering after the deaths of their husbands. The Bible encourages them, "Weep not, Behold the lion of the tribe of Judah has prevailed" (Rev. 5:5).

Jesus is the lion of the tribe of Judah. He has prevailed in the life of the widow. "Do not weep." Jesus encouraged the widow of Nain, who had lost her husband and her only son (Luke 7:11–13).

One day, the widows visited me at home in the Kiambogo village and asked me when the seminar would start the following morning. I told them it was to begin at 9:00 am. They told their friends about it through the phone. Their friends had to wake up at 5:00 am in the morning to prepare to walk more than twenty kilometers. Some of the widows had no shoes but still attended the seminars anyway.

DO NOT WEEP

The purpose of the seminar was to support widows emotionally, physically, and spiritually. The participants were empowered and strengthened through Bible teachings. I share practical principles for living a "set-apart life," which is marked by repentance and humility.

The seminar stirs the hearts of some of the widows who feel stuck in their lives while prompting them to move forward successfully. I teach them simple ways to partner with God by giving their tithes and offerings. In the Bible, a widow was blessed by Jesus for giving all she had in the offering. I urge participants not to be victims of circumstances, but rather to be victors by developing an attitude of thanksgiving to God in their lives. God is faithful!

Widows had testified that they felt revived as the joy of the Lord reigned in their hearts after acting upon the promises of God. They became empowered to start income-generating projects.

After the seminar, widows discover a new life in Jesus. A life full of inner joy, peace, and purpose as they move forward. I remember one widow whose home was built with polythene papers in an open field. She was a hopeless single mother of eight children. After the seminar, she decided to start a small business of selling vegetables in the market. God helped her business until she earned enough money to support her large family. She later bought her own plot and built a house. God is faithful.

Many widows are encouraged in the seminars to face life's challenges. The word of God can allow you to overcome every situation or circumstance in life by faith in Jesus.

I am encouraged by the moving and inspiring testimonies of some of these widows. They say they are built up, strengthened, and empowered. Many of them have improved their lives.

The Scripture tells me to care for the widows. I should be my sisters' keeper and lend a hand with great love whenever it is needed.

"Pure and undefiled religion before God and the Father is this: to visit orphans and widows in their trouble, [and] to keep oneself unspotted from the world" (James 1:27).

The act of praying for the widows is not enough by itself. We should support them spiritually, and even financially if need be. Praying for them alone without showing them love in action is useless.

Jesus wants us to bear one another's burdens. Widows in our ministry, Gospel Messengers Church, are being trained to be Christ's ambassadors.

Some young widows suffer very much when family members fight to remarry them. It's against God's will to force the widow to marry. It is good to let the widow decide for herself how she wants to live after the death of her husband. Some families mistreat the widow and the children of the deceased. We are helping some widows to file legal cases as well as to hire lawyers for their claims of inheritance and properties.

I help to wipe the tears of the widows. One day I remember sharing my vision of reaching the widows with Alice Wanjiku, the wife of Rev. Francis Nganga, the pastor of Gospel Messenger Church, Gilgil Branch. She told me that God was leading her to start a ministry for widows in her church, but she did not know how to go about it. I encouraged her to start with the help of the other two ladies from my church. Her ministry to the widows is now well known in the regional local churches.

One day she prayed with a single lady for her needs. She got a well-paying job in Nairobi. A few years later, when Alice prayed for this lady again, she got a visa to go to America, and she now has a job there.

Another classic example of taking God at His word was when the family of Alice had a dire need for money for their family upkeep. They believed in God for a plot. Alice told her husband that she was going to pray, fasting and alone in the prayer center for seven days. She spoke with God concerning the plot and other needs of the family.

God spoke to her and assured her that her prayers were answered. After breaking the fast, Alice returned home to her husband with great joy because God had indeed answered her prayers. A few days later, God touched somebody who sent her money through her account. The payment was enough to buy a plot and other basic needs of the family. This encouraged her to start a ministry for widows dubbed, "God of the Widows."

The miracles Alice got from God made her vow that she would support the widows in her ministry. God told her to be a blessing to the widows and opened doors for her. Ministering to the widows is her ministry now. Alice encouraged the widows that God hears and answers prayers. With God, everything is possible. Without faith, it is impossible to please Him.

She shares the little she gets daily with widows. Her best friends and children support her in this ministry. She is asking other people to emulate Jesus Christ in support of the widows. Jesus promises to bless those who support the widows and orphans.

Every month, Alice calls the widows into her small house and prays with them as she shares gifts with them. Sometimes she visits them in their homes, reads the scripture, prays, and establishes fellowships with them. Everyone in her area, including the local and national leaders of our church, know her passion for the widows. She has a board of five members who help her in her administration and management of this ministry.

"What do you do to help this ministry survive?" people ask her. She would answer, "It's through prayer and fasting. It involves a close walk with the Lord all the times." Alice is given to prayer and fasting. She makes specific prayers to get specific answers to widows' needs. She has totally committed herself to the Lord and has great compassion for the widows.

She gives to the widows with an open hand and does not take advantage of them. Alice believes that God will supply all of the widows' needs according to His riches in glory. She looks up to the city above, whose builder and maker is God. She prays and intercedes for the widows, asking God to give her willing partners in this ministry.

The question: are you a widow? This book is written to give you hope in your hopeless situation. Are you cast down? Let me revive your spirit by saying, "Weeping may endure for a night, but joy comes in the morning" (Psalm 30:5). Are you suffering and crying because of disappointment in your life? This book will kindle a burning hope in the mind and heart of every widow that has lost hope in this world.

Every needy person, every widow, orphan, disowned child, and drug-addict will find answers for their problems in this book. After reading this encouraging message, you will realize that your hopelessness, fear, and despair will turn into vibrant hope, faith, and restoration. May this message inspire, restore, and motivate you.

Jesus is willing to save, heal, transform, and deliver the hopeless from all of their problems. Jesus is ready to wipe your tears. He can change your weeping into rejoicing. I have seen thousands of hopeless people being given a new start in life after they surrendered their lives to Jesus Christ. Remember. He encouraged the widow of the city of Nain, "Do not weep," because God is "God of the Widows."

Will you support this ministry with your treasures and with your prayers? I offered myself as a sacrifice on the holy altars in the church of Christ. I remain close to the pastors, carefully watching over them and protecting them from false doctrines. I encourage them to protect the flock of Jesus Christ as faithful shepherds.

I taught and warned them about the strange fire, the fake anointing, and the false doctrine. I gave them the living examples of the sons of Aaron, Nadab, and Abihu, who offered strange fire before the LORD, which He had not commanded them to do. "So fire went out from the LORD and devoured them, and they died before the LORD" (Leviticus 10:1–10).

God has given me many pastors in our ministry. Although we have many male pastors, I have done research recently that shows women are becoming qualified enough to hold leadership positions in our ministry.

Allow me to take this time to encourage women in the ministry. Many communities in Africa are refusing women ministers in their localities to teach and preach the gospel. Some spiritual leaders are teaching false doctrines that women should not teach or preach in the church. These fake reasons, family issues, and other false beliefs are hindering women from ministering the gospel.

I am advising ministers that you need to have a calling from God and a vision to start ministering with the help of the Holy Spirit. Another important thing women should have in life is ambition. Ambition is the key to anything you want to do for

Christ. It has brought many mighty preachers to the top. You can emulate wonderful women like Joyce Meyers. Her anointed teachings can lift a woman from where you are stuck to the top. Do not be shy in your village or town; move on by faith.

God is willing to use you when you have self-confidence. Start teaching and preaching; trust God to back your ministry. Be focused and be intentional with your ministry and vision. Put God first before everything else in your life.

Male ministers succeed because they depend on God for everything they do. This makes them very strong in their ministries. You should do the same. Women ministers should take the time to act in Jesus Christ. Do you want a fruitful ministry? Stop depending on others; depend on your God. It's time to stop working for other people's dreams; work on your own.

Don't let anybody make you feel guilty for being a woman, because God has fearfully and wonderfully made you. You are God's vessel. He wants to use you mightily to fulfill His divine purposes in this hurting world. Stick to the ministry that God has called you into, and then, don't let anybody stop you from pursuing it. Don't let anybody intimidate you or make you feel less important because you are a woman. You have been called by Jesus Christ, who has no discrimination whether you are a Jew, a Greek, a man, or a woman. We are one in Christ (Gal. 3:2).

In my ministry in East and Central Africa, I have encouraged many women pastors. I remember one-woman pastor in Elburgon, Mariashoni Forest, Nakuru County. God saved Lilian in Bomet County. She lived with her husband for some years in Bomet and then purchased a five-acre plot in Mariashoni village. That's when God called upon Lilian Kailel to be a full-time pastor in this home village. She is one of the women pastors in our church.

Lillian started preaching to her children, who accepted Jesus Christ as their personal Savior. Her husband who is a police officer also accepted Jesus Christ. They started a church in their home. She would preach the gospel in the village, and even to a small group known as the Ogiek, who are hunters and gatherers in the Mariashoni Forest and the Nessuit Forest in the Mau complex.

This community lives in the forest with their families. They survive by hunting wild animals, collecting honey, and gathering fruits and herbs. The forest is divided into territories for each clan. The clans use streams, big trees, and hills to mark their boundaries. No one is allowed to cut trees or trespass onto another clan's territory. They ignite a forest fire after harvesting honey, take a bath in a sacred well, and harvest honey before the flowers are shed.

These rules are adhered to, and curses are used by Ogiek elders to discipline anybody violating them. For example, the Ogiek men will go hunting while the women gather fruits and vegetables. Collection of herbal medicine is also done by specific older adults with thorough knowledge on how to cure particular diseases using particular herbal medicine.

All children up to the age of 6–15 years of both sexes attend school; classes are mixed ages and abilities. However, the quality of education is low due to inadequate school's lessons are taught in Kiswahili and English.

Lilian has to preach the gospel against all the odds in this community. She has to fight with all traditional beliefs common in the Ogiek, such as early marriages among the small girls. This is also associated with the persistence of female genital mutilation (FGM), especially among these people.

Consequently, girls who have undergone FGM rarely get the chance to complete their education. An Ogiek pastor confirmed that immediately after Ogiek girls undergo FGM, the next step is to get married. More than 98 percent drop from school in class seven and eight to get married.

Generally, the disadvantaged position of women among this community group is further reflected in the access to social-economic opportunities. In education, preference is given to the boy child over the girl child. The negative perception against female children is caused by cultural beliefs in which the Ogiek believe women are for marriage and childbearing. Lillian is called to win the Ogiek to Christ. Please, pray for her.

I am also encouraged by the steadfast faith of Pastor Elizabeth in Timboroa in Eldoret. She is a full-time pastor in our ministry. She started preaching the gospel in this village, but unfortunately, her husband died. She is a widow who is preaching the gospel with boldness to the Kikuyu and Kalenjin communities. Some of these communities have joined her church.

Elizabeth was helped by her son to plant this church, and later her son joined another ministry and left her to lead this local church. Her ministry is well-known in the area, for she ministers and prays for the needs of the villages. God has assured her that He will meet all her financial needs in her life and ministry. She shares what she gets with other widows in the village. God has helped her start a ministry for the widows.

Elizabeth believes that God hears and answers prayers. With God, nothing is impossible! That's why she is asking other people to emulate Jesus Christ in ministering and helping the widows. Every month, she calls all the widows into her small house and prays with them after teaching them the Word of God. Sometimes she visits them in their homes and form fellowships together.

Everyone in the area, and even the national leaders of our ministry, know about her ministry to the widows. When I visited her church, I was very much encouraged by her faithful ministry. I encouraged her to form a church board of no less than five members to help her manage her church.

Other women were asking me how this uneducated woman can manage such a big ministry. I told them that it is through prayer and fasting. Elizabeth lives close to the Lord at all times. She encourages the widows by telling them to be specific in their prayers to God. She gives and ministers to the widows with an open heart.

I'm teaching women factors that can contribute to greatness or success in their ministries and in the church today. Women are worthy of good things in the kingdom of God. Act now!

Let me tell you that the world is expecting you to put aside your fears and preach the gospel. I'm empowering women pastors by trying to remove any barriers that would hinder them from teaching and preaching in the church today. Do not stop serving God, even if the barriers be social, cultural, economic, or spiritual.

My church has a pivotal role to play in empowering women to participate in the ministry as teachers and preachers.

We want widows to participate in small businesses. We train them on how to start a business, and we do so by using cheap materials in basket-making and sewing. This small business can make them self-reliant—this is an essential activity for those living in the villages' slums and ghettos.

We are teaching them how to market their products. The Bible says, "The blessing of him that was ready to perish came upon me, and I caused the widow's heart to sing for joy" (Job. 29:13).

It is my prayer that God will open your eyes to start helping the widows around you. Find your area of ministry, or join us in making a difference in this hurting world. Remember. The mission field is very close to your home. Real love will cause you to do something to help the widows. The Bible says, "May the God of hope fill you with all joy and peace as you trust in him, so that you may overflow with hope by the power of the Holy Spirit" (Rom. 15:13), and "whatever you do, do it heartily, as to the Lord and not to men, knowing that from the Lord, you will receive the reward of the inheritance. For you serve the Lord Christ "(Col. 3:23, 24).

Let's improve the widows' lives, knowing that everything we do for Christ's sake will have an inherent value in our lives. Let's do to others what we would like others to do to us. Let's show love and kindness to the widows from the depth of our hearts. We are encouraging them to make God their only hope in this world. The Bible says to the widows, "for thy maker is thine husband" (Isa. 54:5).

We are teaching the widows about child growth and how to avoid HIV/AIDS, which is the greatest threat in Africa. We make sure that we enhance spiritual as well as physical development by helping the widows work with their own hands. We also teach them the Word of God.

CHAPTER THREE

DANGERS OF FEMALE GENITAL MUTILATION

IN THE WOMEN SEMINARS and conferences, I teach about the dangers of female genital mutilation (FGM), one of the most optional topics. As a women counselor, I have expertise in sex abuse matters and other problems affecting women. I am mostly invited in churches and women forums to speak on this important issue. I don't fear about addressing any of the issues that are affecting women today. There is definitely a great need to share with young people the dangers of FGM. Although this could seem as interfering with matters of other communities and their cultures, let me try to define what female genital mutilation means.

FGM is the cutting of a very sensitive part of the body in the female genitals, known as the "clitoris," for non-medical reasons. This evil behavior is embraced by some communities in Africa as well as Asia. It is deeply rooted in the cultures and social norms of communities that practice this destructive behavior.

In some communities, it is designed to control a woman's sexuality. Most of the affected communities believe that if a woman's genitals are left intact, she becomes too excited sexually to resist sleeping with any men around. There is a very crazy idea, or reasoning, that a woman has to be helped in order for her to remain faithful to her husband by removing the genital part that makes her go sexually crazy.

Another evil grounded belief is that the genitals of a woman are dirty. FGM is meant to remove those dirty parts. These evil beliefs are so strong in some communities that a woman who has undergone FGM cannot get a husband. In one community, men even believe that a woman with intact genitals can poison a man who has sex with her and cause him to die. These are myths!

Although there has been division among clergies on the religious connotations of FGM, some communities believe that it is sinful not to be circumcised. This religious angle may mean that we who are advocating for an end to FGM are interfering with other faiths.

A woman who lives in a community that performs FGM finds herself in a tight corner where she has no other option but to undergo the practice so as to be accepted by the community. One lady from our church was married in one of these communities; she had resisted undergoing the practice. She was trapped when she was giving birth; that's when the women of the community came to assist her. Immediately after giving birth, she was forced to undergo the cut. It was very unfair and unjust to take away her rights and freedoms like this. She cried foul while the whole community celebrated, even the men and young boys and girls.

This evil practice is a very serious gender issue in these days. Spiritually and medically, it has very serious implications. Bleeding, infection, and pain can be so severe it may cause death. Communities have buried several girls after the cut. Some cannot conceive after FGM due to the damage of their internal organs after the procedure. A number of women have pain during sex and will never experience pleasurable sex. Psychologically, the memory of the pain can be externally damaging. If children are circumcised, they immediately live up to the stereotype of women and terminate their education for early marriage.

Recently, I was shocked when a doctor went to court in Machakos petitioning for FGM to be legalized for adult women;

to be done in all health facilities. I wouldn't want to comment with the case in court; the judge made the ruling. The case was defeated and dismissed. Women throughout the whole country were weeping quietly as they did not know how the judge will rule. This is what I'm describing as traumatizing. Some of our members of our churches are living with these consequences feeling as if I'm touching raw wounds. I'm always out there to condemn with the strongest of terms the practice of FGM in our communities.

In my ministry today, I'm teaching women and teens in East and Central Africa. I'm using social media and the Internet to reach them. I'm encouraging them to join the ministry as full-time ministers and overcome the false doctrines that claim that women should not teach or preach the word in the church.

I'm doing a campaign on female genital mutilation (FGM) among some communities that are practicing this evil behavior. I'm doing this campaign in Kisii, Nyamira, Kajiado, Narok, Lamu, Kuria, Samburu, Garissa, and Meru. Recently, I was doing a campaign in Marioshoni to a small group of hunters and gatherers known as the Ogiek. Their community survives by hunting wild animals, collecting honey, and gathering fruits, vegetables, and herbs in the Marioshoni and Naisuit forests of the Mau complex. All children in this small community up to the ages of four and eight of both sexes attend school, with class being mixed ages. However, the quality of education is very low due to the schools being inadequate. Classes are taught well in both Kiswahili and English.

I was preaching the gospel to this community trying to win their souls for Christ. But traditional beliefs, like early marriages among small girls, are very common with the Ogiek. This is also associated with the persistence of female genital mutilation (FGM) among the community.

Generally, the disadvantage position of women among this community group is further reflected in the access to socioeconomic opportunities; in education, preferences given to the boy child as opposed to the girl child. The negative perception against the girl children is caused by cultural beliefs where the Ogiek believe that women are for marriage and childbearing. The girl children are abused as a result.

I'm standing strong in my fight against female genital mutilation in Africa and beyond. Why would you want to die prematurely? Choose life. In this book, I try to share a recipe for victorious living for the youth. The ingredients in it will build up the youth spiritually. In my life, I have been pursuing my lifelong vision of reaching the youth despite the severe pressures of the lusts of their flesh.

God has given me wisdom and revelation on practical ways to support and encourage the youth and women in this hurting world. I like sharing the humorous features in my favorite newsletter, "The Gospel Messenger." In this newsletter, the youth and women can share their testimonies of healing, restoration, deliverance, and salvation. I write about my story of hoe God delivered me from fornication, the lust of the flesh, and drug abuse. I challenge the Christian youth to live out to the convictions they profess. I tell them to stop dating and keep their commitments until the day of marriage.

Some of my favorite topics in the newsletter include courtship and marriage. I encourage youths to never lose hope. I advise them to maintain their fellowship with their teachers, parents, and pastors. The word of God is very powerful, and it can enable them to overcome temptations and the lusts of the flesh. I teach them a hot topic on hope in crises and how to endure hardships until the wedding day.

Many parents, pastors, and teachers have encouraged me to continue with my effective seminars and youth camps. One parent wrote to me, "My daughter was completely stressed out, but now, after the youth seminar, she is fully restored." I tell the youth the importance of saying "NO!" to evil lusts and how to say "YES!" to Jesus. I am planning to build a youth resource centre where youths can get access to Christian books, videos, and tapes with topics that will encourage them.

Write to us for a complete brochure with faith-building teachings. We are receiving overwhelming testimonies from the youth. The word of God encourages me. Jesus is our life. "I have come so that they might have life and that they may have it more abundantly" *(John 10:10)*.

I want you to declare that you do want to have life and that you will have it. "You shall declare a thing, and it shall be established for you so that light will shine on your ways" *(Job 22:28)*. Jesus is the way and the light of the world. I have declared that "I shall not die but I live and declare the works of the Lord" *(Psalms 118:17)*. A warning to the youth is, "For if you live according to the flesh, you will die; but if by the spirit you put to death the desires of the body, you will live" *(Romans 8:13)*.

I want you to choose life. I am teaching on my topic of warning to the youth dubbed "You Will Die." Do you really want to die? Promise me that you will put to death the desires of your body and live. Blessed is every youth who will overcome temptations. "However, each one is tempted when he is drawn away by his own desires and enticed. Then when a desire is conceived, it gives birth to sin; and sin, when it is full-grown, brings forth death" *(James 1:14).*

Mark these words, "You Will Die," if you follow the desires of your flesh. Call Jesus now, and He will deliver you from drug addiction and sexual abuse. Read my books, "The Gospel Messenger," "Love Without Lust," "Never Lose Hope,"" I Shall Not Die," and "Kill Me Not." Hope For Survival, and Do Not Weep! You will learn how to receive eternal life and how you can maintain it forever!

CHAPTER FOUR

COMPASSION TO THE LESS FORTUNATE

GOD IS GOOD TO THE poor, the needy, the hungry, the orphans, the widows, the sick, and the destitute. "This I recall to my mind; Therefore, I have hope. Through the LORD's mercies, we are not consumed, Because His compassions fail not. They are new every morning; Great is Your faithfulness" (Lam. 3:21–23).

Caring for the needy or the poor is an often tiring and sometimes thankless mission. The problems of hunger and poverty continue to hover like plagues in Africa, despite our efforts to relieve them. However, God's compassions never fail. They are made new every morning. Each new day we have new compassion to minister to the less fortunate. Despite our feelings or fears, we are strongly empowered by the Holy Spirit to continue serving the less fortunate in our local communities and on the national level.

We volunteer to meet their needs, even the ones living in remote areas. We meet some who are at their wit's end, without anything to eat and with no solution for their problems. They are destitute. We give them hope so that they can cope with their terrible situations.

As their lives lie in ruins and all they have longed for is lost, we tell them there is still hope. We let them experience the forgiveness of God for their sins. For each loss, we minister comfort. For their fears, we give them resources for new strength. For their failures, we advise them to try again. For each tragedy, victory by grace. For each disappointment, encouragement. When the lives of people have been shattered by hunger and threatened by poverty, we volunteer to support them with new compassion. "Whoever shuts his ears to the cry of the poor will also cry himself and not be heard" (Prov. 21:13).

We have helped the less fortunate who are living in great distress. Some have long-term burdens and problems that are too heavy for them to bear. Have you ever seen people begging for daily bread? We care about people's plight, especially those who are overwhelmed by enormous problems in their lives without the essentials for survival. Compassion is loving, combined with actions.

"In those days, the multitude, being very great and having nothing to eat, Jesus called disciples to him and said to them, 'I have compassion on the multitude because they have now continued with me three days and have nothing to eat. And if I send them away hungry to their own houses, they will faint on the way; for of them have come from afar'" (Mark.8:1–3).

We have compassion for the less fortunate. Let us have food bank contributions in our churches and ministries. Let's organize charitable groups to support the poor, the needy, and the less fortunate in our communities. Human life is vulnerable to pain, suffering hunger, poverty, and oppression. People are living in real suffering and hopelessness. Africa is full of many people bearing weighty burdens. Through the newspapers and T.V. screens, we see the different expressions of hunger, civil wars, fear, poverty, and despair, dramatically conveying the hopelessness in this chaotic world.

The gospel is about the love and the compassion of Jesus Christ to human beings. We are to reflect on his teachings in the Bible. His love is taking new dimensions as applied today. We must show practical love to those who are suffering. Love must touch the poor, the needy, and the less fortunate in this world. We must reach those who are suffering from diseases and HIV/AIDS. Love must reach the broken-hearted, heal the hurts in the soul, and touch the dilemmas in our lives.

Each time we use the love of Christ to heal the broken world, we find new ways to reflect it. We act as good stewards by sharing God's love and our resources with others. God's love is unconditional; it is not dependent on our wills or even on our desires. Jesus said, "Love one another." No excuses for not loving. We must love just as Jesus described, "A new command and I give you. Love one another" (John 13:34). We are to love even the unlovable. He renews us every day, so we have the power to obey his command to love. We are to show our new compassion, new love, and new kindness to the entire world and the less fortunate around us.

When King David wanted to show kindness, love, and compassion for Jonathan's sake, he asked if there was anyone left from the house of Saul. Ziba told him of Mephibosheth, a son of Jonathan, who was lame in both feet. David showed the kindness, love, and compassion of God to this lame man. "And David said to him, do not fear; for I will show you kindness for the sake of your father, Jonathan and I will restore to you all the land of Saul your father; and you shall eat at my table always" (2 Sam. 9:1–7). We show kindness, love, and compassion to the poor, the needy, and the less fortunate for Christ's sake. We are reaching the hurting in Africa.

You becoming involved in the lives of the less fortunate means a sacrifice on your part. We are living in a world where people don't want to be inconvenienced, but life takes on a new meaning when you invest it in others. You can give without loving, but you cannot love without giving.

Let us see the needs of others through the eyes of Jesus Christ; let us answer the cry of the poor, the needy, and the less fortunate in this life. "Use worldly wealth to gain friends for yourselves, so that when it is finished, you will be welcomed into eternal dwellings" (Luke 16:9) When we use our resources to help others, especially to communicate the gospel, we reap eternal dividends. God wants us to be generous in meeting the needs of others. Riches have eternal value only when we use them to bless those in need.

Life in this world is not permanent. It is fleeting, and death comes to us unexpectedly. Do something to bless others before it is too late. We should treasure every soul in Africa. This is my prayer for all: "May the God of hope fill you with all joy and peace in believing, so that you may abound in hope by the power of the Holy Spirit" (Rom. 15:13).

Our mission is to give hope to the hopeless in Africa. The Holy Spirit fills us with joy, peace, and hope. God's love in our lives is more powerful than all of the evil forces in this world. So, when we hear people are suffering from misfortunes or tragedies, we rush immediately to give them hope. Hope is the best gift to the suffering. We desire for the entire world to know Jesus Christ so they receive eternal life, joy, peace, and hope.

Let the sufferings and anguish in your life bring you to the end of your resources and get to know your creator, the Almighty God. We are messengers of HOPE. "Do not fear those who kill the body, but cannot kill the soul, but rather fear him who is able to destroy both soul and body in Hell" (Matt. 10:28).

There is no one who is hopeless whose hope is in God. I am a messenger of hope. Many people in Africa have little reason to go on living. God is using us to bring the message: there is still hope for them. They feel that they are about to die. But today, people of God have sustained them. Don't give up in despair; remind yourself of God's goodness and love. Talk to him; He is good and will meet your needs. He'll lead you in paths of joy, blessings, and new hope in your life. Beyond your losses and despair, there is new hope that is going to be born in your heart.

Because God is living, you will live. God has a wonderful plan for you. In this changing world today, you can trust the unchanging God. "Blessed be he of the lord, who has not forsaken His kindness to the living or the dead" (Ruth 2:20). Genuine love always manifests itself in kindness. This truth is vividly portrayed in the book of Ruth when Boaz saw Ruth gathering grain behind the reapers in his field. He commanded them to help her. To her, this was a blessing from the lord.

In the same way, the people whose lives we touch will also experience God's love through our compassion and generosity. We should ask God to give us opportunities to show kindness to the less fortunate in life. That is Christian love in action. If you know the Lord and love your neighbors as yourself, you, too, will be generous in your giving. Do a deed of kindness to anyone in need? Compassion is the oil that can take all the friction out of life.

In Africa, millions of people are living in fear because of the increase in the mass destruction of life by famine, civil war, tribal clashes, floods, disasters, calamities, and HIV/AIDS pandemics. The devil has developed strategies for destroying and killing us before we even know Jesus Christ as our personal Saviour. He is causing fear to oppress them. Fear is a tormenting spirit which the devil uses to keep many people bound and hopeless. Fear causes you to feel discouraged, disappointed, weak, ashamed, condemned, miserable, and defeated. God says, "For I, the LORD your God, will hold your right hand, saying to you, 'Fear not, I will help you'" (Isa. 41:13).

God has given us a burden to minister hope to all those who are suffering. God will never give us a responsibility greater than we can bear. In our ministry control office in Nairobi, we have a humanitarian project that is involved in ministering to the hungry, the poor, the needy, orphans, street children, widows' inmates, and those fighting with an HIV/AIDS pandemic.

CHAPTER FIVE

FIGHT AGAINST HIV/AIDS PANDEMIC

EVERYWHERE IN THE WORLD, people are lamenting because of the high degree of sexual insanity in these last days. Every day, millions of people are perishing without hope, not knowing which way to turn for help. In both urban and rural areas, people are plagued by sexual immorality. Fornication, prostitution, and adultery are resulting in many people testing as HIV/AIDS positive.

In our cities, you might be surprised to see young schoolgirls engaging in prostitution. Some of these girls become pregnant as soon as they reach puberty. I am concerned, as one of God's ministers, when I meet with these girls at night as they roam the streets half-naked and looking for clients.

We also find that some of the girls are being physically abused.

This gives a clear picture of the 21st-century world with its depravity and increasing rape attacks. Today, sugar daddies are defiling young schoolgirls. This fact has dramatically hindered the education of the girl child in Africa and has resulted in many cases of abortion as well as an increase of illegitimate street children.

Our ministry has a project in which we organize mobile clinics to minister to all those who are bound in drugs, alcohol, and prostitution. We also do counseling for people living with HIV/AIDS. We preach Christ to them because it is only Christ who can heal, deliver, and save people from incurable diseases and sins. We work with a team of committed Christian doctors, nurses, social workers, and volunteers. We go into the inner cities, slums, and ghettos, as well as the rural areas.

We have full-day counseling programs for the victims we counsel. We preach and pray with families, youth, and singles who are living with dangerous viruses. Some victims are living with stress, anger, and temper, as well as broken hearts and visible wounds to their bodies. We counsel with husbands, wives, girls, and boys who have been sexually abused or physically battered by their mates. We minister to parents who are suffering with pain in their hearts due to the death of their rebellious sons or daughters. Widows are suffering due to the deaths of their husbands.

We have discovered that there is no pain more severe than the HIV/AIDS virus. It keeps the whole body of the victim burning with pain everywhere. As I write, we have millions of people living with the virus today. The virus causes the body to be very weakened, and the victim feels very lonely, ashamed, and unwanted. Many victims die from the spirit of regret in their hearts.

Our ministry of counseling is very effective in healing the broken-hearted and of relieving the pain in their aching bodies. We lead the victims to the one who is "called Wonderful, counselor, Mighty God, Everlasting Father, Prince of Peace" (Isa. 9:6). I have seen Jesus Christ heal the bodies of the victims and restore them spiritually. Just like medicine, the word of God heals many physical problems. It's only by the word of God, which had been sent from above to cure every disease and problem in one's life.

"He sent his word and healed them, and delivered them from their destruction" (Ps. 107;20).

"Bless the Lord, O my soul, and judged not all his benefits: Who forgives all thine iniquities; who seemeth thy life from destruction, who crowneth thee with loving kindness and tender mercies" (Ps. 103:2,4).

Through His word, which is like a sharp sword, He pierces through our sins, iniquities problems, and diseases as He saves us from ALL of our sins. His word is like a seed that bursts into a new life. It is like a lamp that shines for us in the darkest nights and shows us the way. It breaks through our lives like a hammer breaking a hard rock into small pieces, burning away every evil thing in our lives. It is a fire that cannot be quenched. It is like a mirror that shows us how we truly look.

That's why we use His Word in the counseling in our ministry. The Word has caused many to be healed, delivered, restored, and saved. Many people have been broken of bad habits, drug abuse, alcoholism, and prostitution. Many people have overcome temptations in their lives through the Word.

Question: Do you have any problems in your life now? Do you have any hurting, bleeding wound in your heart? Do you have spiritual or physical problems? Do you have some nameless grief? A pain that is making you sad or sorrowful? Some unexplainable ache in your life and soul? Come to Jesus Christ with all of your sins, diseases, pains, aches, sorrows, grief problems, and burdens. He will give you rest; "Come to me, all who are weary and burdened, and I will give you rest. Take my yoke upon you and learn from me, for I am gentle and humble in heart, and you will find rest for your souls, for my yoke is easy and my burden light" (Matt. 11:28,30).

Rejoice that we have a caring Father like this. He is the one who gives us rest in our souls. He is willing to provide for our lives. We are part of His flock, so we can say, "The Lord is our shepherd. God is ready to pour healing oil of the Holy Spirit to heal all your deep hurts. For I will restore health unto thee, and I will heal thee of thy wounds, saith the LORD" (Jer. 30:17).

Jesus is willing to heal and to save you now. Do you want to be healed and born again? I am pleading on behalf of your soul to the throne of grace. Let this be a word in time and receive Jesus as your personal Saviour. Join a good Bible-believing church and start serving your God.

You must understand and have a clear picture of the eternal suffering and pain caused by the burning fire in hell. Hell is forever. The word of God says hell is not made for you. It was prepared for the rebelling angels. However, people will go there if they do not accept Jesus Christ as their Saviour. The horrible picture of hell will make you decide to receive Jesus as your Saviour now. Jesus is coming soon! The hour of His coming is at hand. Surely it is your time to seek Christ to save yourself now because that is when you shall be saying peace and safety; "Suddenly destruction cometh" (1 Thess. 5:3). Fear not, only believe!

Medical science has failed to provide treatment for HIV/AIDS, but Jesus heals every disease.

HIV/AIDS PANDEMIC

WE ARE LIVING IN THE most terrible days. Every day we are constantly disturbed by what we read in our daily newspapers and see on television. Many hopeless people are really in danger of becoming depressed and losing all hope for survival.

An epidemic of incurable diseases plagues the world. Sexual immorality and sexual perversion are directly responsible for the HIV/AIDS epidemic that is killing millions of men and women. Many marriages and families are perishing because of the sexual insanity of our days.

The problem is the same in both the rural and urban areas. Parents are lamenting because many young schoolgirls are becoming pregnant when they are still children. We have many cases of abortion, rape, prostitution, and homosexuality. Everywhere we turn in Africa, there is moral decay, and so, there is suffering all around.

You see, there is turmoil in our continent today. Families are living under severe pressures. The reason many husbands are running away from their families is that they cannot meet their responsibilities at home. Failure to meet their obligations means that they lose their authority as heads of their families. That's why some husbands are looking for prostitutes who can put them up in their houses. This is what families are battling against in Africa.

Many people, especially those living in the slums, are being plagued by the HIV/AIDS pandemic. We have said that we, as a ministry, are not going to remain silent and maintain a "holier-than-thou" attitude while people are being destroyed by the pandemic.

We have declared to fight a life-and-death battle against this plague that is killing millions of people. Today, many people are engaging in risky sexual relationships. For these reasons, many families are being destroyed. In every corner of the world, there are cases of untimely deaths caused by the HIV/AIDS pandemic.

We are living in the evil last days of a fallen and chaotic world. We are working to stop the spread of this dangerous epidemic. We are campaigning by telling people to abstain from illicit sex. We are trying to save as many souls as possible. We are teaching the community about the dangers caused by risky sex behaviors. We are appealing to our beloved government, NGOs, and willing people to help us in this life-saving project in the ministry.

We sorely need moral and financial support because although we have the experience and expertise to make sure that the victims can access medical drugs and spiritual help in the ministry, funding is required to provide these services.

The Bible tells me, "Blessed is he who considers the poor. The Lord protects him and keeps him alive; he is called blessed in the land, thou dost not give him up to the will of his enemies. The LORD sustains him on his sickbed, in his illness thou healest all infirmities" (Ps. 41:1–3).

Nations are lamenting because of the high degree of sexual perversion. Nations are perishing without hope, not knowing which way to turn. I feel concerned when I see young girls roaming the streets looking for clients. You could find hundreds of half-naked girls being abused sexually in the streets at night. This is a picture of the 21st-century world, with its increasing rape attacks and sexual abuse. Jesus is the answer to this hurting world.

COUNSELING

WE HAVE COUNSELING programs to minister to the needy as well as all those who are bound by drugs, alcohol, or prostitution. We also do counseling for those who are HIV positive. We preach the gospel to them because we know that only Jesus Christ can heal, save, and deliver them from all these problems in their lives. We have seen Jesus heal diseases and save radical criminals. We work with a team of committed Christians, social workers, nurses, and doctors. We go into the inner cities, slums, and ghettos in villages, as well as the rural areas.

We have found the ministry of counseling to be very effective in healing the brokenhearted. We have rescued many from life's problems. We are leading all victims to the one who is known as "a wonderful counselor the mighty God, the everlasting Father, the Prince of Peace" (Isa. 9:6).

Jesus Christ is the wonderful counselor, and He can restore you spiritually, mentally, and physically. Jesus can heal all incurable diseases and all problems in your life today. Why don't you call on Him now? You will find what your heart has been longing for. Jesus is the answer.

The word of God is near to your hurting soul. Only the word that is sent to you from Heaven can heal you. The Bible says, "He sent his word and healed them, and delivered them from their destruction" (Ps. 107:20).

The word of God is like a mirror that shows you precisely what you look like. That's why we are using the word in counseling. We have seen people being saved, healed, and delivered from different circumstances. We have seen many people with very bad habits; young men who had been living like beasts have been changed by the ministry of counseling and are now living good lives.

These are the last days, and cities, towns, and villages are in the hands of demon-inspired youth. These are the signs of the crooked and perverse generation, as well as the fulfillment of the end-time prophecies. We trust the Lord to help us in this counseling ministry. We appreciate the combined efforts made by Mr. and Mrs. Ken Taylor, the missionaries from the U.S.A. They have been supporting our projects in the community.

We have assisted the poor and HIV/AIDS victims by giving them basic survival requirements. Together we have been helping many who are yearning for liberty from sins, drug addiction, alcoholism, diseases, joblessness, hopelessness, and economic woes, as well as those who are suffering from deep feelings of emptiness in their souls.

These missionaries have been visiting our village often with their mobile clinics. During the rainy season, they have been using their double cabin and four-wheel vehicle. After serving the community with their health care services, we would take them into our home where they could relax while eating our African-made meals. In the morning, we would take them for a short walk around the village where they could meet and chat with children and adults.

On Sundays, we'd invite them to our church service where they could enjoy our moving workshop. In the service, they would become very excited and participate in our worship, praise, clapping, dancing with joy and celebrations with the beating of the drums. After the service, we would bid them farewell until another visit. We thank God for these people of God who have been assisting us practically to make a difference in this hurting world. God bless their work.

Our ministry is setting the captive free and breaking every yoke of the devil in the lives of sinners and the oppressed. The Bible says, "Is this not the fast that I have chosen: To lose the bonds of wickedness, to undo the heavy burdens, to let the oppressed go free, and that you break every yoke? Is it not to share your bread with the hungry, and that you bring to your house the poor who are cast out? When you see the naked, that you cover him, and not hide yourself from your own flesh? Then your light shall break forth like the morning, your healing shall spring forth speedily, and your righteousness shall go before you. The glory of the LORD shall be your rear guard. Then you shall call, and the LORD will answer; You shall cry, and He will say, 'Here I am'" (Isa. 58:6–9).

You can volunteer to work on this project for the needy. Why don't you write for details? We are soon planning to expand into Nairobi, Eastern, Northeastern, Rift Valley, and the coastal regions. You can help us in providing medical care, childcare relief, and pastoral care in the community. Send your donations to "Stay Up Rehabilitative Community Based Organization," a community-based organization (CBO) registered with the Ministry of Culture and Social Services to minister to the needy, the poor, and the hopeless.

It gives me great pleasure to serve the destitute, drug addicts, alcoholics, prostitutes, criminals, and HIV/AIDS victims. As a Christian organization, we are committed to serving the needy. We are redefining our mission statement to focus on these emerging issues that hurt many people and are causing untimely deaths. I want to achieve my divine dream of giving hope to the hopeless. Many are facing an uncertain future because they lack the basic necessities for survival. Like Jesus, I have compassion for all those who are suffering.

We are deeply involved in fighting AIDS. At first, our pastors thought that AIDS was always the result of sexual immorality, so they shunned all those who were infected. This included the members of their churches. They labeled them as sinners who were somehow beyond the forgiveness of God. After teaching them the facts on AIDS and how Jesus cares for ALL of the suffering people today, they obtained a better understanding of how HIV is passed from one person to another. Our pastors have greatly improved, and they are now personally involved in fighting this pandemic.

We have Christ's mandate to reach the unreached. The purpose of our church is to play a role in reducing the spread of HIV/AIDS. As church leaders, we are teaching our members the dangers of this pandemic and how to avoid infection. This is one of the most important things that our church is doing. We are teaching our members to know why God created us and how we can live in him. We are asking them to support and pray with those who are infected, as Christ himself would have responded to people who are victims. We are setting an example for our pastors and members of our church as we encourage them to be willing to be tested in the VCTs! We advise them that early detection and counseling are vital in helping the victims. We counsel families on how to live positively with the victims. We organize mobile VCTs in communities where they cannot usually access this service. Those who are tested are given sympathetic and godly counseling confidence.

We are training many counselors in the church, and especially the pastors, about HIV/AIDS and how to handle the victims (PLWHA). We teach our counselors how to visit the sick at home, how to pray for them, and how to invite them to church, for they are part of the community. We show them practical love as we introduce them to Jesus Christ, who died for their sorrows, grief, sickness, iniquities, and sins. Victims ought to know that Jesus Christ loves them in their predicament. We are making a difference.

God is the only hope for the hopeless. He is ready to save and heal whoever comes to Him in whatever state he or she could be in. We ask our pastors and members to help the victims in giving them food, water, firewood, clothes, and money for medication. They can also help them in cleaning their houses or washing their clothes (Isa. 53:4–5).

We invite the victims into the church to hear the gospel and our testimonies. The church is their greatest source of hope, encouragement, and comfort.

We encourage the victims to join our faith-based organization (FBO), so they can be guided through this project. Income-generating projects can benefit them by working together with others in making baskets, knitting, farming, raising livestock, and beekeeping. They can get money after marketing their products to cover their day-to-day needs at home.

We are also teaching the youth. We have noticed the young people, especially girls, are vulnerable to HIV infection. We are trying to address this issue in youth meetings and camps. We are teaching them about healthy marriages. We are also targeting schools and colleges. We are teaching the young people biblical subjects on risky sexual relationships, peer pressure, and purity through the word of God. We use published booklets, articles, poems, dramas, posters, tracts, videos, and articles that teach about HIV/AIDS. We encourage them to live godly lives. We are planning to hold seminars in schools and colleges soon.

In rural areas, we are advising the communities to use qualified doctors, especially during circumcision, instead of using risky traditional methods. We have helped many in the rural area by providing them with doctors and sanitary venues for circumcision. We greatly discourage any cultural practices that involve the youth in sexual intercourse after circumcision.

We teach the rural flock what the Bible says about sexual immorality and the importance of marriage. We discourage all traditions involving sex outside marriage. We explain how to avoid sexual immorality, even in the church.

We discourage all the traditions of wife inheritance and the traditions of marrying many wives. We teach the importance of faithfulness in marriage. We discourage the abuse of drugs and alcohol because they reduce people's ability to control themselves against sexual immorality that may result in HIV infection.

We have full understanding and compassion to minister to the needy, and especially the people living with HIV. Many people in rural areas, even church leaders, have been opposing us because of our involvement in fighting the pandemic. Many church leaders do not understand the topic of HIV/AIDS, so they cannot help us in fighting it.

We are leading by example, and that's why we are willing to help in curbing this pandemic. When Jesus comes, He will be interested to know how many needy people we have helped. He will ask us how many orphans and widows we have ministered to; that is why we have a great need to respond to this global problem of HIV/AIDS. As gospel messengers, we are on the front lines in this battle. I believe when Christ said that we are to be the salt and the light of the world, we are to be doers of the word.

We are trying to rescue many people from the cruel hands of the devil, who is the cause of all the problems and evils in the world. Many are suffering and crying from inner grief because of the depression, which comes because of HIV/AIDS pandemics and the resulting stress in the lives of the victims.

I have personally met victims who are very frustrated and desperate; victims who have reached the point of thinking about committing suicide to escape problems and shame. Many have lived with the virus without knowing it, but the stress and anxiety is still evident in their lives. I have met victims who are suffering from many family problems, emotional struggles, and economic problems. They feel that there is no way out. They find the world to be crumbling around them, and they are unable to bear another agonizing day. They become so physically and emotionally exhausted that they lose hope for survival.

Some young people are at the point of wishing to end their lives because of drinking and drug addiction. Many of them are depressed because drugs and alcohol have blinded their minds, causing them to lose hope and purpose in life. They feel their only option is to commit suicide and spend the rest of eternity in hell. The devil is getting people deeper and deeper into darkness until there is no hope for them. The devil affects their bodies, souls, and spirits until they have no way out. Jesus is the only hope for them.

CHAPTER SIX

MINISTERING IN LOVE

WHEN I TOLD OTHER CHRISTIANS about God speaking with me about starting a ministry for the needy in the village, they thought that I was crazy. Little did I know that God had called me into the ministry mainly to meet human needs. I started with a simple and humble beginning. I was a simple preacher in the village. Other pastors overlooked me and underrated my ministry.

My first priority was to win souls for Christ, and secondly, to meet the needs of the hopeless. I was to reach out in love. I was called to serve and do good to others without drawing attention to myself. I started with the immediate needs of those who had been very close to the church. My ministry was rooted in a deep love for the needy.

I used most of my time to visit the sick at home and in the hospitals to minister hope to the needy in Jesus's name. I encouraged the helpless and the suffering. As a servant of God, I was willing to go out to meet other people's needs.

I served all without asking anything from them or their tribes. I had offered my life completely to God. I have nothing in this world that I call my own, for everything I have is God's. My life belongs to God. I am fully devoted to God. I was praying for God to give me direction in this ministry. I wanted to serve others in need so that when Jesus comes, He will tell me "Well done, good and faithful servant" (Matt. 25:21).

My service included every act of love, mercy, and kindness to others. No matter how small my service to others was, I wanted to reflect on God's love. I will never lose the capacity to serve the needy. God has helped me remain in the line of my call. I will use my life to serve others.

One Scripture that has encouraged me is the parable of the good Samaritan, the person who shows love by mercy in action. Like him, I want to serve the needy in the village and the city. I will not be sidetracked by people. I want to use my time to serve others, rather than discussing things with people who have no action. Faith without works is dead. Let's put our hearts and hands together as we go out of our way to meet the needs of the hopeless.

The world around us is full of needy people who are waiting for you and me to do something to help them. I am called to bring radical changes to the lives of the needy. I feel concerned when I see the needy suffering without hope. Instead of moving with the crowd, I will show practical love, mercy, and kindness to the hopeless.

I show the needy the way, which is through Jesus Christ. I know some people, and even some nations, spend billions in money trying to solve their problems, yet their efforts turn out to be in vain. Nations fail because they are dealing with the symptoms of their problems, while the root cause is left untreated. What can we do with our problems? Let's all turn from sin and come to Jesus, who has all the answers to all of our problems.

I like ministering to the needs of people despite all that I have been facing, as I have been experiencing God's love in this ministry. God has been encouraging me. My friends and relatives have been sending me encouraging letters, and they assist me when I am down or under pressure.

The Bible tells us that God is love, and it's in His nature to love us. He did not send His Son here to earth for the righteous, but rather for the sinners. "God shows His love for us in that while we were sinners, Christ died for us" (Rom. 5:8).

Jesus made friends with sinners, unclean people, tax collectors, and prostitutes. God's love is self-sacrificing. There is no greater love than this: somebody dying on the cross for sinners. God's love is very different from what human beings regard as love. God's love is agape love. It is a pure love. Human love is based on feelings and emotions. God commands us to love even our enemies, and even to help them in times of need. After understanding God's agape love, our hearts are filled with eternal love, which flows from the throne of grace. We love people, whether they love us or not. God's love makes us act lovingly to the needs of others.

Jesus not only taught love, but He also showed love to us. He showed His wonderful love by doing good and helping the needy. He saved, healed, and fed the hungry. He restored sight to the blind and touched lepers to heal them. "By this, we know love, that He laid down His life for us, and we ought to lay down our lives for the brethren. But if anyone has the world's goods and sees his brother in need, yet closes his heart against him, how does God's love abide in him?" (1 John 3:16–17).

Christ's love means being unselfish and thinking more of the needs of other people than of our own needs. Christian love means putting the needs of others before your own needs. "You shall love your neighbor as yourself" (Lev. 19:18). My heart is the center of God's love in my life. God's love manifests itself in my life, making me completely wedded with Jesus Christ.

The Bible says that "Though I speak in tongues of men and of angels. And though I have the gift of prophecy and though I have all faith, so that I could remove mountains. And though I bestow all my goods to feed the poor, and though I give my body to be burnt, but have no love, I am nothing. Love suffers long and is kind; love does not envy love does not behave rudely and is not proud and thinks no evil. Love hears all things, believes all things, hopes all things, endures all things, and love never fails" (1 Cor. 13:1–8).

Because God's love is working in my life, I don't have to force myself to help others or to do good to the needy. It happens naturally. God's love makes me focus on spiritual matters. It makes me receive everlasting blessings by doing good for others. Love does not make me be puffed up, but rather it makes me humble and kind to others. God's love makes me reach out to the needy. I don't strive to get material things, but I cheerfully give my life to serve others. "My little children, let us not love in word or in tongue but indeed and in truth" (1 John 3:18).

My prayer is that God may open my spiritual eyes to see the needs of other people around me. I want to see the needy through the eyes of Jesus Christ. God gives wisdom and strength to fulfill my vision. I'm willing to go deeper and deeper into God's love and compassion. I'm making a difference in this hurting world. I remember what Jesus told a man who was set free from demonic powers: "Go home to your friends and tell them what great things the Lord has done for you" (Mark 5:19).

That's why I am always busy telling my friends and neighbors about the great things that the Lord has done in my life since the day of my salvation and deliverance. I use my God-given gifts and talents to reach the unreached. I believe the mission field begins at my doorstep. I am a channel of God's love to this hurting world. My mission is alive when I meet the needs of others. The Bible says, "Whatever you do, do it heartily, as to the Lord—knowing that from the lord you will receive the reward" (Col. 3:23, 24).

DO NOT WEEP

My goal is to save everyone from perishing. This ministry gives me great satisfaction. I know that although the world seems to be advancing in science, it has failed to provide comfort to millions of souls who are perishing and starving for the word of God. I preach the word of God because I know I can give hope and inner peace to the hurting.

I do good to others because a good deed done in God's way and in God's time can bring satisfying results. Even a little kindness to a needy person is like a life-giving cup of cold water to a thirsty person. It has eternal value because it is done in God's name (Mark 9:4). If you want real satisfaction in your life, trust in Christ, and then go and do something to please Him.

Let's be like the early Christians, who gave generously to the Lord and supported the needy. Their hearts always overflowed with God's love and goodness. So, let's be generous with our resources, and the mightiest kind of giving will come from the depths of our hearts.

I am living in this chaotic world where millions of people are living in fear because of civil wars, strife, conflicts, earthquakes, disasters, calamities, diseases, and the mass destruction of HIV/AIDS pandemics. Everywhere in the world, people are living in fear because of terrorists. The Bible says, "Perfect love drives out fear" (1 John 4:18).

God loves me. I remember the day when God manifested His wonderful love and care in the lives of my family and me. That day, my little daughters were playing their usual hide-and-seek game outside the compound. I was talking to the in-laws who had paid us a visit. Our daughters were heard shouting and playing outside as we were talking inside the house with our guests.

Suddenly we heard crying and screaming outside. We rushed out quickly. Our daughter was crying out in great pain. When I checked, one of her legs was broken. Soon I remembered the little daughter of the ruler of the synagogue who was reported dead. And Jesus said, "Fear not, only believe." This scripture encouraged my heart, and we prayed. After prayers, I rushed her to the hospital. The prayers controlled her pain until we reached the hospital; she had received strength to overcome the pain.

I carried my daughter to the doctor. The doctors worked very quickly, and in a very short time, my daughter was admitted. The doctors treated her by putting a cast on her broken leg, then she was discharged. We paid the bill as we left the hospital, and she thanked all the doctors and nurses who had tended to her. She encouraged them to remain faithful in their service to the needy.

I thanked God for His love and protection. Our inner life and peace were not overwhelmed by this great trial in my family. God gave us the grace to overcome the temptation to panic.

We thanked God together with the doctors in Kijabe Hospital and left for home, rejoicing. God's practical love and care were manifested in our family. God is good to all those who trust and wait upon Him. God turned a bad story into a victory for our family. One month later, we revisited the doctor for a checkup. My daughter's cast was removed. Her leg had healed. To God should all the glory be given!

Everybody in our family has a living testimony of God's practical love and healing power. Everyone thanked God for our little daughter, who kept her faith in the storm. She testified of God's love and healing power to the doctors and nurses who had tended to her. During the whole month, she made everybody, including other Christians, see Jesus in her story. Jesus cared for her in the traumatic days of her life.

After this tough period, she received new strength and would lead us at home with very moving songs of praise about God's love and faithfulness. She likes praise songs even today. God is a loving shepherd in her life. The promise is, "I will bind up the injured and strengthen the weak" (Ezek. 34:16). This is one of her favorite Scriptures. She praises the living God, who helped her at a tender age.

I thank the members of our family for their moral support and their prayers during this time in our lives. It is my prayer that my family will continue to support other needy people around them. God is good, for, "He heals the brokenhearted and binds up their wounds" (Ps, 147:3).

I also thanked my friends, like Rev. Mwai, for giving me his car to travel to and from the hospital. Christians and relatives waited for us at home, and we praised and thanked God together for answering our prayers by healing our beloved daughter. Praise God!

Everybody at our home was very excited as they joyfully worshipped and praised God. Many Christians and relatives spoke at our thanksgiving meeting and encouraged my daughter for having endured great difficulties. This experience helped to make my daughter, as well as the entire family, very strong spiritually. God is good all of the time.

This was a very shattering experience for us. We were troubled on every side, but God was with us in all things. I could not pretend that everything was okay, as some people may do in this situation, but I remained very open about this particular situation. We experienced the love and presence of God in this situation. As I opened my heart to God in prayer, He took my troubles, problems, and trials away with Him.

He released His healing power to my daughter. I was overjoyed and shared my testimony with other Christians. To me, this was a miracle. I do believe that God heals the brokenhearted and binds the wounds of the weak. God is good to us, and that's why we minister to Him in love.

CHAPTER SEVEN

SHARING JESUS WITH THE NEEDY

I HAVE BEEN REACHING out in love to hurting souls for more than thirty years. My whole life is wrapped up in sharing Jesus—His power—His compassion—His wonderful words of eternal life and abundant provision. The promise is, "For I will restore health and heal your wounds" (Jer. 30:17).

Today, more than ever, I am using all means to heal this high-tech society with the gospel of love. I am giving the hopeless and struggling people God's hope and restoring hurting souls. You need Jesus! You can experience His love, salvation, restoration, and goodness. I could tell if one is injured and wounded.

That's why I have made a bold stand to preach the gospel of love and hope to this hurting world. My ministry is for demonstrating God's redeeming love and salvation to the needy. I am proclaiming the truth to all people from all walks of life. Could you please join me in restoring hurting souls across Africa? I am asking you to get involved. Share with me your love, your prayers, and your financial support.

I believe that God's love will arrest you, and you will possess God's promises in every situation in your life. Jesus is going to touch you, and you will experience a deep sense of fulfillment and joy in your life. You need Jesus to save you from this evil generation. I pray that God is going to give you His riches and blessings in your life. I am a gospel messenger. I preach hope in this hurting world, just as the prophet, Isaiah, had written: "Look, I am sending my messenger ahead of you, and he will prepare your way" (Mal. 3:1).

I teach the hopeless and the needy to wait upon the Lord in all things. I advise them not to wait until they are desperate before they try to trust God. I tell them to trust in God with their whole being.

God has given me the wisdom to help the needy. He directs me in all things in the ministry. You cannot make good choices in your life without God's help. Don't depend on your own understanding. Trust in God, for God is our creator and our Savior.

God is our provider, and He cares for our lives and needs. God has good plans for our lives. God's ways are best. So, let us not ignore His existence. He is alive. I experience His power and presence in the ministry. I know He is alive.

Let us seek the Lord in our lives. Let us ask Him for direction. I have a living picture of my ministry. That's why I want to serve the Lord with my life and ministry. I know that my redeemer lives. He gives me all the things I need in life and for the ministry. The Holy Spirit helps me to overcome situations in the ministry. I know that it is God's will that I may preach the gospel of hope to the needy and the hopeless.

I encouraged and comforted a widow who was walking along the road accompanied by her children. She was weeping for her husband, who had been killed in tribal clashes. The widow had experienced the traumatic loss of her loved one. "My husband died," she cried. "Don't cry," I comforted her, my voice going out to this hopeless widow. "Jesus is your answer in your hurt."

The Bible gives us hope. They praised God, saying, "A mighty prophet has risen among us," and, "God has visited his people today" (Luke 7:16). When life brings nothing but rejection, misery, and pain, it's easy for the victims to doubt that God really saves and heals people. What are you expecting in life? God is willing to save and heal you. Open your heart to Him now and say to Him, "Save me, God!"

God is waiting for you to call upon Him. Will you? He is looking at you with a smile on His face. He loves you, and He wants to save and heal you now. Jesus knows of your sins and the problems in your life today. Do you ever think of Jesus? He loves you and wants to open your eyes so that you can see His power and love in your life. Jesus is all you need. Never underestimate His power and love. He is willing to save you. Call on Him now, and you will see the difference. Jesus loves you.

After your salvation, you will keep on reading the word of God and keep on meditating through the word of God. Meditate on certain verses in the Bible, and then you will have success in your life.

I practice what I preach. I preach hope and love to the needy and hopeless. Trust God in this hurting world. Trust God, for he knows all of your problems, and He cares about you. Believe His Word and His promises in the Bible, and you will live. All things are possible with God. I am regarded as a messenger of hope. My ministry is a symbol of hope.

I encourage the needy and the hopeless as I assure them that their problems will be solved and their needs met. The Lord commissioned me to reach the unreached and give hope to the needy and the hopeless.

I have achieved many things through faith power. I learned to saturate my mind with the Word of God. I allow the Word of God to reign in my heart and to recondition my personality.

My life has been changing day by day. I encourage the hopeless by reading to them, "Now may the God of hope fill you with all joy and peace in believing that you may abound in hope by the power of the Holy Spirit" (Rom. 15:13).

I am an achiever. The Word of God has modified my life and my mind. This allows me to receive what the Lord has promised in His Word. The Bible teaches me how to receive the promises from God. "If you can believe, all things are possible" (Mark 9:23). "If you have faith, nothing shall be impossible to you" (Matt. 17:20).

I believe the Word. It has the power to build my faith, which moves mountains in my life. The Bible says, "If God be for us who can be against us?" (Rom. 8:31). I personalize this Scripture in my heart by repeating, "If God be for me who can be against me?"

I expect God to give my family food and security. And by picturing the power of God, I receive positive results. I acquire new courage, new faith, new power, and deeper confidence. Every day I expect the best, and with God's help, I can attain it. Do not believe in defeat, because there is nothing impossible with God. My eyes are firmly fixed on my source of power. Through God's power, I can do all things. The Bible says, "The secret things belong to the Lord and God, but those things which are revealed belong to us and to our children forever so that we may do all the words of this law" (Deut. 29:29).

So, I had to find God's revealed will in His Word, and now I have hope for my future. I know my responsibilities. My duties are spelled out in the Word of God. The more I study the Word of God, the more I know God's will for specific situations in my life. The Bible does not tell me how much money I will use for the ministry or what program I will make. It does not tell me what I will do on Monday or Saturday.

However, it does tell me what the will of the Lord is. "So be careful how you live. Don't live like fools, but like those who are wise. Make the most of every opportunity in these evil days. Don't act thoughtlessly, but understand what the Lord wants you to do" (Eph. 5:15–17).

I pray, and the Word lets me know the will of God. I have also learned much by reading books and by listening to other gifted teachers of the Word. The final word always comes from the mouth of God. God has everything I need for my ministry. I seek God when I face complex situations. I like feeding my inner man with true doctrines from the Word of God. I make enough time to read the promises of God in His Word.

The Holy Spirit leads me to the right promises which fit certain situations in the ministry. He helps me to develop a godly common sense in making decisions. I make the right decisions and obey the Word of God in my life. The Word transforms my mind, and it gives me direction in all situations. The Word gives me options and unique ideas on how to solve problems. I follow what others are doing in their ministry, but I always depend on God to lead me.

As a pastor to the needy, I give them hope and counseling. I use all of my abilities and talents to meet their needs. God has prepared and equipped me in this ministry. I evaluate myself to find what I'm required to do, and then I make decisions that have a positive spiritual, as well as a positive physical, effect on the well-being of the needy.

I don't do things alone in the ministry. I don't want to be a lone-ranger, so I have a team of mature spiritual people who assist me. I appreciate their wise decisions and their ideas on simple or complex issues. I learn much by listening to their good suggestions. The Bible says, "The way of a fool is right in his own eyes, but he who heeds counsel is wise" (Prov. 12:15).

Sometimes my teammates can see what I cannot see, and they can be more objective in their evaluation of issues and situations in the ministry. They sometimes correct me by pointing out errors in my judgment, and they add valuable insights. Sometimes I find them to be more knowledgeable than me on specific issues. I cheerfully receive contradictory advice as I decide whether or not the advice is worth listening to. I always accept those with reliable information concerning some topics.

Not only do I need information, but I also need godly counsel from spiritual people who are in tune with God. I ask for help from my coworkers with an open heart. I am ready to be corrected and persuaded to rethink my initial decision. I like doing research first on issues in the ministry before asking for advice from others. The Bible says, "For it is God who works in me both to will and to do His good pleasure" (Phil. 2:13).

God encourages me in the ministry. "The diligent lead surely to abundance, but everyone who is hasty, comes only to want" (Prov. 21:5). I don't make haste in doing things in the ministry. If I am extremely uneasy about a decision, I take time to evaluate why I feel that way. In some cases, I may lack peace, but I exercise my faith in God according to the examples provided in the Word. In Acts 6:2–4, the early church was very willing to meet the needs of the needy by distributing food to them. This example has moved me to volunteer to do the same for the needy. I have presented my body as a living sacrifice to God. God's will is what is best for my life. I have helped many to find salvation, deliverance, healing, and a new start in life. It is my joy to serve the needy.

Human beings are vulnerable to pain. I answer the questions that are commonly asked by the hopeless and the needy in life. Thousands of people are living in terrible situations without food for their families. It is only Jesus who can save such perishing souls. Every needy person is thirsty for something he or she does not have in situations that are beyond his or her control. Every day those people's hearts are hurting and bleeding. They need encouragement in their lives.

I have met hopeless people who ask, "What should I do in my life? Is there hope for me?" I give hope to these people who are at a crossroads in their life and don't know which way to turn for help. Many such people are living with no hope for the future, and they are numbed by the present. Some of these people need life-sustaining supplies and the Word of God. Can I be contented to remain inside the church building when people are crying for help on the streets? I must extend the love of God outside the church walls. People outside are waiting for God's love displayed through our actions.

I will never be ashamed to give what little I have to the needy. I will always remember the old woman in the Bible who was offering to God the little she had. Jesus considered her offering as very valuable in the hands of God. God is increasing my resources as I share what I have with the needy. I am a good steward of whatever He gives me to share with the needy.

I know that it is God alone who has a lasting solution to every crisis of the needy. It is God alone who can banish suffering, pain, famine, and poverty from people forever. I am a living letter that speaks of our Lord, Jesus Christ. I am called to comfort and encourage the brokenhearted, the sorrowful, and the grieving.

I know that a good deed to the needy is like medicine for their souls. I know that it is good to be faithful with little things first, and then God will increase your resources and your responsibilities. You must show accountability for every penny that is given to the needy. God has assigned me a ministry to the needy. I speak hope to the needy, and the works of this ministry is like a sweet-smelling fragrance to those in need.

God has given me a dream for Africa because our continent is vulnerable to many dangerous calamities from diseases, famines, floods, civil wars, and conflicts. Millions of people are suffering and crying in great pain as others are dying without hope. The voice of God has an irresistible divine power in it. This power made me develop a burning passion for helping the needy. I was to preach the wholesome word of God, as well as all of its power, with conviction to the hearts of the hopeless.

The gospel message has touched and changed many souls. My dream was birthed in prayer, and it is sustained by faith and sparked by the Holy Spirit. What we are doing today is but a drop in the ocean of Africa's needs, but we are winning people to Jesus with others in love. Our mission is to restore hurting lives. God is love.

CHAPTER EIGHT

I HAVE COMPASSION

I HAVE COMPASSION FOR the poor, the needy, the hungry, the orphans, the sick, and the widows. Jesus met people's needs at every meeting. One day the multitude was very great, and they had nothing to eat. Jesus called His disciples to Him and said to them, "I have compassion on the multitude because they have now continued with me three days and have nothing to eat. And if I send them away hungry to their own houses, they will faint in the way, for many of them have come from far" (Mark 8:1–3).

Let us be like Jesus and have compassion for the needy and the less fortunate. We must act with God's love and support people with significant problems in life. We should help our neighbors who are infested with drugs, crime, or teen pregnancy, street children, and all those who are messed up. The Bible says, "In a surge of anger I hid my face from you for a moment, but with everlasting kindness, I will have compassion on you says the Lord your redeemer" (Isa. 54:8).

Think of what God sees as He looks at the dirty sins that people are doing in Africa. He knows of all the evils, which are against His will. He sees right into our hearts as the Scriptures say: "From heaven, the LORD looks down and sees all mankind; from his dwelling place he watches all who live on earth—he who forms the hearts of all, who considers everything they do" (Ps. 33:13–15).

God sees us all. God sees the drunkards and the drug abusers. He sees the rapists and murderers sinking downward to hell. He knows of all sins, additions, bondages, depressions, and rebellions. He feels compassion for all who are suffering. God sees the prostitutes who sell their bodies. He sees all those sinners who treat sex like just another sport. He sees people misusing sex in this world and spreading HIV/AIDS to others. He sees the millions of abortions happening to babies daily. He sees married people breaking their vows by having sex outside of their marriage. Despite this, God has compassion towards such a self-destructive society.

God sees the gays and lesbians. He sees people who are doing things that are an abomination to Him. He sees people suffering and dying from different kinds of calamities and crises. He sees bishops and pastors committing sexual sin with Christians in the church. He sees millions who are dying of HIV/AIDS. He sees people pretending they obey when they suffer from the pandemic. The death toll is rising every day, yet people do not seem to worry.

God has compassion for the suffering. God sees people obsessed with the lust of money— those who lie and cheat to get more money. He sees churches wandering away from the truth, which is revealed in the Bible. He sees pastors and preachers who do not preach the truth about holiness and repentance. He sees those church leaders who are involved in sexual immorality and therefore don't care for the disadvantaged people. How can God not get angry with such evil behaviors of such leaders, you may ask?

God's wrath against sin and those who rebel against Him is rising every day. When we do wrong, God gets angry, yes. However, He would rather see them repent of their sins than become lost forever. The Bible says, "Do I take any pleasure in the death of the wicked? Rather, am I not pleased when they turn from their ways and live?" (Ezek. 18:23).

Compassion literally means to suffer with someone. Jesus suffered with us and for us. The Bible says, "My heart is changed within me; all my compassion is aroused. I will not carry out my fierce anger, nor will I devastate Ephraim again. For I am God, and not a man—the Holy One among you. I will not come against their cities" (Hosea 11:8–9).

Even though God has compassion for the needy, He is angry at our sinful condition. In fact, He's more than just angry. God is furious. His wrath blazes hot against all evil. His entire, infinite being is literally and absolutely opposed to all wrong. God looks on sin with sadness, but He has deep compassion for the misery that afflicts the needy and less fortunate. God loves you.

Are you sexually promiscuous, and your doctor told you that you are HIV positive? That you are going to die of AIDS and have probably already infected other people with the virus? God feels compassion for you, so repent of the sins you have done. He cares for you. He has given your life and everything good that you have in the same way a parent provides care and provides for a child. As God created us, we are essentially God's children. So, when you disobey God, he reacts as a parent would. He is angry when you rebel against Him. He sees you destroying your life in sin, and He sheds tears of compassion. God cares for you. "It is of Lord's mercies that we are not consumed because His compassion fails not. They are new every morning" (Lam. 3:22–23).

Let me say that although famine and poverty continue to hover as plagues over Africa despite our efforts to relieve them, God's compassion fails not. They are new every morning. Each new day we go out to minister hope to the hopeless. Despite our feelings and fears, we are powerfully empowered by the Holy Spirit to continue serving the needy in our local communities, and even to the national level. We minister to those in very remote areas who are at their wit's end. We will give the needy hope. Many can cope with their terrible situation because of hope.

We lead many to experience the forgiveness of God. Those who claim they are failing in life are advised not to lose hope. We tell them to try Jesus. For those who are disappointed, we encourage. The Bible says, "Whoever shuts his ears to the cry of the poor will also cry himself and not be heard" (Prov. 21:13).

We are ministering to those who you may have seen desperately begging for bread, as well as those people living poverty-stricken lives without the essentials for survival. We are caring for their plight and especially those who are overwhelmed by enormous problems in their lives. Compassion is love in action. Let's have food bank contributions in our churches and ministries. Let us organize charitable groups to support the needy in the cities and the rural areas.

In Africa, millions of people are vulnerable to hunger, poverty, oppression, and hopelessness. Through the newspapers and television screens, we hear terrible stories of civil wars, famine poverty, and despair. The media is conveying the hopelessness of this chaotic world dramatically.

Despite the bad news, the gospel teaches us about God's everlasting love and compassion. God's ministry is for showing practical love. This wonderful love is touching and changing the lives of people, even those who are infected with HIV/AIDS.

God's love is touching the brokenhearted and those with dilemmas. We have many ways to express God's love to the needy. We want to remain the stewards of God's unconditional love, which is not dependent on our own will nor desires.

David wanted to show this unconditional love and kindness for Jonathan's sake, so he asked if there was anyone left from the family of Saul. And there was in the house of Saul a servant whose name was Mephibosheth, a son of Jonathan, who was brought before King David. He was lame, but David showed him love, kindness, and compassion. He welcomed him to eat at his table despite his terrible condition. David said to him, "Do not fear, for I will surely show you kindness for Jonathan's, your father's, sake and will restore to you all the land of Saul, your grandfather, and you shall eat bread at my table continually" (1 Sam. 9:7). This is what we are called to do. We are to show love, kindness, and compassion to the needy and the less fortunate. We are called to touch the hurting in Africa.

I know that being involved in such a ministry means great sacrifice. We are living in a free world where we don't want to be disturbed. However, life takes on a new meaning when we invest in the needy. Let me say that you can give without loving, but you cannot love without giving. We see others' needs through the eyes of Jesus Christ. Hear the cry of the poor, the needy, and the less fortunate. Jesus said, "I tell you, use worldly wealth to gain friends for yourselves so that when it is gone, you will be welcomed into eternal dwellings" (Luke 16:9).

God wants us to give generously in meeting the needs of others. Riches have eternal value only when you use them to bless the needy. Remember. Our life in this world is temporary. Death comes unexpectedly. Let's work to bless others, and especially the needy. Let's treasure every soul in Africa. Our mission is to give hope to the hopeless. Hope is the best gift to give to the suffering. We have given hope to all those in despair—those who feel they are about to die. I advise them to believe the word of God, which says, "I shall not die but live and declare the works of God" (Ps. 118:17).

In the book of Ruth, you can read the story of Naomi and her daughter-in-law, Ruth. They were poor and hopeless when they returned to their land after staying in a foreign country for many years. Boaz saw Ruth gathering leftover grain in his field. He gave her enough grain for their survival. They blessed the Lord, saying, "Blessed be the Lord who has not forsaken His kindness to the living and the dead" (Ruth 2:10). God is good all the time to the needy. I have a dream for the needy in Africa. I have compassion (Mark 8:1–3). God has given me a vision of reaching the unreached and giving hope for survival to the hopeless.

The Needy

WE HAVE A CHRISTIAN way of reaching out to the needy through love because we are members of Christ's body in Africa; we are Christ's hands, feet, and mouth. Jesus meets needy people through us. He saves, heals, and comforts the suffering through our mouths. He lovingly touches them using our hands. Although we cannot solve all the problems in this world, we are called to give ourselves to help the needy. Jesus wants us to show mercy to those in need. The Bible says, "For I desire mercy and not sacrifice" (Matt. 9:13).

We are called to minister to the whole man, spirit, soul, and body. We are encouraging our ministers to become involved in communicating the need for physical and economic development. In Africa, some church leaders believe that physical development is nonspiritual and worldly. Jesus is the light of the world in all things.

We are called to care about the welfare of the needy in our society, whatever their needs. We are chosen by God to be channels of blessings to the needy. We are to allow God's love to flow to others by acts of mercy. God has promised abundant blessings to all those who minister to the needy.

The mission field starts at your doorstep. True compassion is love in action. Let's just do it. God's love is not our emotions; it is doing something caring for the needy, not just preaching anointed sermons to them. It means helping them, spiritually and materially, in love. "Owe nothing to anyone—except for your obligation to love one another. If you love your neighbor, you will fulfill the requirements of God's law" (Rom. 13:8).

By ministering to the needy, we have seen God changing a heart from evil to good. Changes in behavior begin with a change in heart. We give the needy the word of God. We pray with those who are in pain. Wherever we go to minister, we see the evidence of the Word changing people and leading them to become good Christians.

Some people come for prayers in our office, and after seeing God answer their prayers, they invite us into their homes to share the Word with their families, friends, and neighbors. After the meeting, some of these people receive Jesus Christ as their personal Savior. We are very thankful to God because after we minister to them, they welcome us into their homes to explain the gospel of Christ to other needy people. We minister, comfort, and encourage many with different needs in their lives. We share the gospel with people because we know that many ministers do not want to minister to people with life's greatest needs and problems. Jesus ministers to all people.

We work with willing people, NGOs, churches, ministries, and donor agencies. Our goal is to take the gospel of love to the needy, and we kindly ask others to do the same. The gospel has taken us to diverse locations because we have agreed to serve all of Africa's people, even those who live in remote areas of Africa. We organize self-help projects for the underprivileged youth, and we sponsor needy students with school fees or scholarships.

We provide wheelchairs to thousands of disabled people to help them move about without assistance. We are dedicated to serving people with disabilities and enhancing their quality of life. We believe that if people with disabilities are given support, they can become successful and productive citizens.

The Poor

OUR MINISTRY HAS DECIDED to take immediate action to alleviate poverty and improve the living conditions in the slum areas. We are committed to providing the basic necessities of survival to the slum dwellers. That's why we are making a charitable appeal to all those who are willing to sponsor or assist us in fulfilling our vision. We are called to do our best to convert love into action.

Do you know what a slum is? Have you ever visited a slum area? If you could just visualize the picture of the life of a slum dweller, you would quickly do something regarding them.

Let me briefly explain to you that a slum is an area where thousands of poverty-stricken people live together in a big village that is in deplorable conditions. These people live in the unhealthiest, uncomfortable, and dangerous conditions. Many of the slum dwellers are jobless, and they struggle hard to provide for their families.

In every corner of the village, you meet with some of these out-of-work, pale-faced, ill-nourished, stunted people. You can see children playing in the streets yet hear the young children crying in the homes for a lack of something to eat.

It is very dangerous for a stranger to walk alone in a slum area because of the threat of attack by gangs of drug-addicted criminals who walk around the area doing demonic activities. Because of these evil gangs, you can sense danger in every corner of the village. Drug abuse and alcoholism are affecting the minds, the feelings, and the imaginations of the victims, causing them to hate, fight, rape, steal, and commit awful crimes. The people live there in fear. Everybody in slums, even the children, has a terrible story to tell about his or her life.

Real problems stem from the heart. Although we are living in the most sophisticated society of information and high technology, our national reputation is marred by problems of racial prejudice, addiction, abuse, divorce, and sexual immorality. Our problems are rooted in the heart because of our ignorance, and this problem has been passed from generation to generation. This is the reason why Jesus Christ said, "For out of the heart proceed evil thoughts, thefts, false witness, blasphemies. These are the things which defile a man" (Matt.15:19–20).

The evidence of the gospel of Christ is what is needed in the slum areas. It is the gospel that can answer all of the life questions which may be asked by the slum dwellers. The most common question is about unwanted children.

This is a severe problem in the slums. Many consider the birth of a child as a problem or a burden in life. Some children are treated as unwanted; they are abused, unloved, and rejected. They end up in the streets where they would become dangerous and a burden to society. The cause of these unwanted children in the streets today is the rampant abuse of sex. Because people have children without planning, it is devastating because the children become a burden. We should consider every child in the family as a blessing. It is better to have only the number you will be able to handle so you will have control over your family.

The other major problem in the slums is the problem of abortion. Many people do not know the difference between abortion and birth control. Abortion is the act of destroying the life that already exists in the womb, while birth control is your decision to not bring a new life into being. We, as Christians, don't encourage the killing of the unborn—abortion is immoral and murder. We need to have a sense of respect and care for each child that is born into this world.

Don't you realize you were brought by God into your mother's womb? What if you were killed in the womb? Why then should you encourage the death of another unborn person? Praise God that you were born. King David said, "For you created my inmost being; you knit me together in my mother's womb. I praise you because I am fearfully and wonderfully made; your works are wonderful. I know that full well" (Ps. 139:13–14).

What a miracle that occurred when you were born, and it is the same miracle that happens every time God brings another new-born child into this world. We should ask ourselves what we are doing to care for each child that God has made and is alive today.

The slum dwellers are human beings, and so they thirst for more answers than this life can offer. Everybody there has an inescapable longing for something this world can never satisfy. There is an intense emptiness in their souls. They are looking for answers as they try hard to fill their inner void with alcohol, evil music, crime, and sexual relationships. That's why we are building churches in these areas. It is only Jesus who can satisfy the human longing in one's soul. We are building an office to assist us in reaching these hopeless lives with the gospel of love before it is too late. We are doing our best to achieve our goals.

Firstly, we are to gather facts to help us proceed with the process of analysis, and secondly, we are to gather materials to build a church and an office. We have discovered that to simply just give the slum dwellers material support is not enough. They need something more in their lives that money cannot buy—they need Jesus, who has a new and everlasting life. It is only Jesus who can make a lasting change in the lives of such people. A change in behaviors begins with a change in the heart. We are trying to positively frame this project to the slum dwellers to arouse their attention.

We have discovered that some evangelical churches have ignored the slum dwellers. That's why we are taking the gospel directly to them. We are not only helping people to overcome poverty but also to help them find new life through Jesus Christ. All the activities of the project include an evangelistic witness with our volunteers, missionaries, pastors, and other Christian workers. We go from house to house with the gospel of love. We are very committed to winning many souls for Christ.

We give free Bibles to those poor families who show an interest in the gospel but cannot afford to buy a Bible for themselves. We look at people with the eyes of love, as every human being is considered God's creation and endowed with equal rights to life's abundant provision, irrespective of race, colour, or geographical location. Genuine love always manifests itself in kindness and mercy.

Will you join us to alleviate poverty in the lives of the slum dwellers and introduce them to Jesus Christ, who died for them? Let's live outside of our comfort zones and help those who are suffering in the slum areas. Give the little you have, and in the hands of God, it will multiply for the needy. In the hands of the needy, a small gift will be considered very big. Don't be ashamed to give a little, because it means a lot. "I was a father to the poor" (Job 29:16). Give in the name of Jesus and remember Mary, who anointed the head of Jesus with the little costly oil that she had. She gave what she had, and though it was little, it was considered very great.

Give the needy at least some of life's necessities. Nothing is impossible with God. He is our provider of all the resources we need in life. So, don't be afraid to share them with others in need. "Have you seen anyone perish for need of clothing or any poor without covering?" (Job 31:19). God is willing to use you for His divine purposes if you are willing to share with others whatever little He has given you. Be a good steward of whatever He has given you.

Just begin to give sacrificially; give until it hurts a little. This is sacrificial giving. God will miraculously increase your gift as you share it with the less fortunate in life. We are messengers of God's love in this world.

We know the short-term relief of which we give to the poor by distributing our little resources is not enough. We must give them the gospel, for it has all the power to change their lives for the better. The gospel gives them direct contact with the living God. In this world, we are like a sweet-smelling fragrance to the sinners. We are living letters that speak well of our Lord, Jesus Christ. A good deed is like medicine to the poor and the needy. An act of mercy to the needy speaks more eloquently than empty words. We are giving hope to the hopeless, bringing them into the presence of God, where they can find new life, joy, and peace. In Jesus Christ, they will find real satisfaction, and their souls will never thirst or hunger anymore. Let's be honest with the little things and show accountability for every penny that God has given us.

God is working generously as we give help to the needy. The Bible says, "Therefore, as we have the opportunity, let us do good to all" (Gal. 6:10). Now that you can visualize the actual situation of the poor and the needy in the slum areas, could you tell your friends and others about it and be willing to join us in making a difference in this hurting world?

Your finances will help us build this project. Join us, and together we shall form a strong crusading army of Christ, marching through the continent of Africa with all the required ammunition to fight all the forces of evil, sin, disease, and poverty in the lives of the troubled.

This is a wonderful story with a strong appeal in it, which is made by a messenger of hope. All my life, I will echo the cry, "Africa for Jesus!" Let it be your cry, too.

CHAPTER NINE

HOPE FOR THE HOPELESS IN AFRICA

I AM A MESSENGER OF Christ sent to preach hope to the hopeless in Africa. I thank God that I am called to preach hope in these end times, when famine, tribal clashes, civil wars, and economic uncertainty are roaring across Africa. I am called to preach to people who are living in despair and desperation. I continue to preach when there are conflicts between neighboring tribes, clans, and nations.

People are living helpless and hopeless lives. In the midst of great destruction and affliction in Africa, I sow hope in the hearts of people. All human anguish, suffering, pain, and turmoil can be traced back to when Adam disobeyed the voice of God and sinned. He was cursed, and this curse was passed to us from generation to generation.

"The Lord saw that the wickedness of man was great in the earth and that every imagination of the thoughts of his heart was only evil continuously and the lord was sorry that he had made man on the earth, and it grieved him to his heart. In those days, only one man and his family did the will of God. But Noah found favor in the eyes of the lord" (Gen. 6:5–8).

We are living in a world full of evil people whose primary desire seems to be to kill others, but may you want it to be different?! How do you cope with the evil people around you? We are now in the hands of demon-possessed people who seem to drag us to degradation as they try to dominate us. Every day we have growing evidence of more emerging evil in the whole world.

However, let's not talk about the evils of others, but rather ask ourselves, "Who will save me from this sinful nature into which I was born?" Sin is the cause of your present troubles, pains, and suffering. "Behold, I was brought forth in iniquity, and in sin my mother conceived me" (Ps. 51:5). So, stop blaming others. Blame yourself for your sins. Do not provoke God to destroy you, "For there is not a just man on earth who does good and does not sin" (Eccles. 7:20).

Remember that you might be the cause of your present problems as well as being the cause of other people's problems. I am saying that sin is the cause of your problems today because I know it. I have been a pastor for some years in the hardest place in the world. The area where I was ministering was plagued with a high crime rate, including stock theft. The residents of the area, including me, coped with hardships. There was no running water, so we had to travel for miles to find water. The roads were impassable during the rainy season, so it could take many hours to ride in an old Matatu over a distance of forty kilometers from the Nakuru Town to our village. There were neither telephone services nor electricity.

I had started a small church where I had been busy conducting a service every Sunday. I had held many open-air meetings in various locations. Souls were saved, and the church had increased in number.

But then, suddenly, tribal clashes erupted, disrupting life in the whole area. There were battalions of armed warriors going to the villages, destroying the houses with fire and stealing personal possessions and livestock. In a few moments, crying, weeping, and screaming filled the air. Because the residents were caught unaware, the only option was to escape with their families to find refuge in the neighboring school. In the midst of this terrible situation, God provided protection and strengthened the residents. Because of prayers, only a few people in the area were injured. There were no reports of anyone losing his or her life. In the neighboring villages, there were reports of mass destruction and mass deaths.

After one week, the clashes ended, and we peacefully returned to our homes. These tribal clashes were caused by greedy politicians who wanted to demonstrate to others their prestige, hate, and lust for power.

But God intervened, and everything became calm. Some of life's greatest tragedies are caused by evil politicians with impure lifestyles. They are corrupted leaders who have offered their lives as a sacrifice to the devil. They desire to kill others in order to achieve their goals. God is faithful and calls us to minister new life and new hope to all people in Africa. Africa belongs to Jesus! I went on with my mission of preaching the gospel. Many of the people of this area were wounded, some emotionally, and others were living in fear, but it was thanks to God that many were saved. "For godly sorrow produces repentance—but the sorrow of the world produces death" (2 Cor.7:10).

My friend, guilt feelings in your life can destroy you. Let God, through the Holy Spirit, minister forgiveness in your life, and you will note that your sins become blotted out. We have been ministering hope and forgiveness to the victims of these tribal clashes. The devil had created feelings of rejection, worthlessness, and emotional scarring in people during the clashes. But by God's unconditional love, they came to feel accepted again. They went on with devotions and fellowships as usual.

God accepts us because Christ pays the penalty for our sins. He clothes us with His righteousness. I release the spirit of God, which sends conviction into people's hearts, leading them to constructive changes in their lives. Conviction of sins and godly sorrow produces repentance. The burden of guilt is made gone, and your conscience is set free. Satan makes us miserable through conviction, but God makes us happy through confession.

I thank God that where I ministered, I could make sure that even the unbelievers knew that God is real. Through prayer, the residents of the villages did not revenge themselves against evildoers. Revenge was defeated. I worked for God in a place where the forces of darkness had a stronghold. I thanked God that through powerful spiritual warfare against the spiritual forces of darkness, I had victory. I was able to pull down strongholds, and I had a breakthrough in the ministry and finances, praise the lord! All those village warriors who wanted to train young boys to fight were defeated, and they returned the boys to work.

We are the light of the world. We are to minister to all those who are affected by tribe clashes or civil wars in Africa. Many are affected physically, emotionally, and spiritually. We advise the victims to cry to God in order to find peace and the assurance of forgiveness for their sins. That way, they'd be able to enjoy life again. For those who are damaged, we give them hope. God loves us very much and cares for our restoration.

Many people in different parts of Africa are suffering as a result of civil war. We have images of exiles and refugees haunting us through the media. Their expressions of hunger, fear, and despair are conveyed dramatically, highlighting their helplessness of being victims of suffering in a chaotic Africa.

Recently in our office in Nairobi, we received a report of refugees who came from neighboring countries. Millions of innocent people are displaced because of civil war or tribe clashes.

Good people who had been living peacefully in their beautiful houses with good-paying jobs now find themselves fleeing to other countries as refugees begging for the basic necessities for survival. We are trying to help alleviate their suffering. We have the responsibility of preaching the gospel of love, peace, and hope to our brothers and sisters by being a member of the worldwide family of God.

We share words of hope in their lives. We do this through our loving witness, service, and care for all in need. God helps us to help others and to reach out to the exiles, the hurting, and the lonely around us. Our mission is to tell them that there is hope. "Say to those who are fearful heart, be strong, do not fear! Here is your God" (Isa. 35:4).

Some say that "home is best." A home is a place where you live with love, joy, and peace with your family. It's where you build up, nurture, and strengthen each other emotionally, spiritually, and physically. Just try to imagine yourself being an exile or a refugee with no safe home again, uncertain of what you will eat. You wander, being isolated and lonely.

Every day you seek a safe place for your family. Imagine yourself passing through the streets of a town with your family having to work hard for a place to live. Your heart may be troubled in exile, but remember that God will never leave you nor forsake you. He is always there to help you and comfort you in your troubles and in times of your greatest pain or suffering. There is hope, as "You have been my defense and refuge in the day of trouble" (Ps. 59:16).

If you refuse to receive the love that God is showing to you now in life, then after your death, which will come to you suddenly, where will you spend eternity? God has promised to save our lives from sins, pains, troubles, sufferings, and tears. "But, God will wipe away every tear from our eyes; there shall be no more death" (Rev. 21:4).

This is in heaven, but where shall you spend eternity? I am talking to you personally in your restless condition. Search until your heart finds rest in God, your creator. He cares for your life now and after your death. He can lead you out of exile into a new life, a new hope for a new beautiful home in heaven forever, where you shall never cry or die. You will live forever. He has given you a wonderful invitation. "Come to me, all who labor and are heavy laden, and I will give you rest." The Lord has promised to carry away all your tears, pains, troubles, and sufferings, "For my yoke is easy, and my burden is light" (Matt. 11: 28–30).

Jesus Christ is always ready and willing to save you from your present condition, and he will send you back to your home refreshed. Are you feeling alone, rejected, or deserted? Many of us have experienced those feelings in our lives, but thank God today that we are restored and refreshed. God has good intentions for your life, even though the enemy has flooded our lives with many confusing and troublesome situations.

Satan wants us to fail to understand God's will in trying moments in our lives. Sometimes God is preparing us for a spiritual work and a better life in the future through our troubled situations. It might seem frustrating, but remember Joseph in the Bible. God was ever-present in every trying moment in his life. God was ready to save, protect, and guide him; He is a good and caring God. "For I know the plans I have for you, says the Lord, plans for warfare and not for evil to give you a future and a hope" (Jer. 29:11).

Although God has good plans for us because he is the Good Shepherd, don't forget that the devil is a thief whose goal is to steal, kill, and destroy (John 10:10). The devil is stealing, killing, and destroying millions of lives through diseases, famines, floods, tragedies, earthquakes, tribal clashes, civil wars, HIV/AIDS epidemics, bomb blasts, and nuclear weapons.

We are messengers of hope, preaching the good news about God's mercies and giving hope to all those who are traumatized by wars, conflicts, and bomb blasts. We save many from the wrath of God, which is coming to evildoers and sinners. The misery you are exposed to now is very different from that which the Lord will inflict at the end when He openly shows His wrath to all those who decided to reject Him on earth.

This is the time to receive God's mercy, forgiveness, and salvation. God's wrath has been passed from generation to generation. Indeed, let every sinner, oppressor, abuser, and victimizer be warned. The righteous "Judge is standing at the door" (James 5:9). "What will He say on the judgment day? Who will rescue them from the coming wrath?" (1 Thess. 1:10).

God is willing to pardon any repentant sinner. The remission of our sins comes after receiving Jesus Christ as our personal Savior. Every believer who trusts Jesus is given immunity from eternal punishment.

There is hope for even those who hate themselves because of the evil they have done to others. We can all find forgiveness before our loving father, no matter what we have done. Through all generations, God has shown us His love to set us free from sins. He has made us understand the wages of our sins and the terrible consequences of our willful disobedience.

We find forgiveness before our God, even when our emotions make us feel as if we have gone very far away from Him. God forgets our past sins even when our guilty conscience makes us feel as if we want to die. God can forgive a mass murderer or a terrorist, for all sins are equal and similar. Some people think that some sins are greater than others, but there is no difference. "For the wages of sin is death, but the gift of God is eternal life in Christ Jesus our Lord" (Rom. 6:23).

Without God's forgiveness, everyday life could end up in despair. Every repentant person can find inexhaustible waters of life in the presence of a loving God. Repentance means a change of actions to receive an overwhelming sense of God's holiness through Jesus Christ.

Our sins are paid in full. The issue of our sin is settled by Christ, and our case is closed. God will not open the files of our guilt anymore. "There is therefore now no condemnation to those who are in Christ Jesus, who do not walk according to the flesh, but according to the Spirit. For the law of the Spirit of life in Christ Jesus has made me free from the law of sin and death" (Rom. 8:1–2). Remember that although King David was found guilty of adultery and murder, he was forgiven.

Paul was killing Christians but was forgiven. Paul was forgiven and called in the ministry. It is God alone who can forgive. In my Christian ministry, I have met preachers and Christians who preach huge, overwhelming waves of condemnation to others but do not preach love, peace, forgiveness, and hope. I don't condemn others. I have a life and death battle for the souls of men.

Keeping myself prepared to preach hope in such a modern society can be an immense battle, but I am always ready to face the mighty battle to get men's souls saved. Memories are important, whether positive or negative, as they all teach us wisdom for the present and give us insight for the future.

CHAPTER TEN

JESUS THE PRINCE OF PEACE.

EVIL BEHAVIORS IMPACT the family unit, causing misunderstanding some members, especially the widows. I'm helping many widows to know the truth to escape from hopelessness in Jesus's name. I am on a mission to help many troubled people turn their lives around before it's too late for them.

I am a messenger of hope in this hurting world. To achieve my dream of giving hope to the hopeless, "Stay Up Rehabilitation Community-Based Organization" was registered so as to give them strategies for effective income-generating projects. We teach them about micro-entrepreneurial involvement and give them skills on needs-based development using our seminars. We are living examples of how these proven-effective techniques can transform the lives of widows. These life-changing techniques have helped many of them to escape from depression, stress, anxiety, fear, suicidal thoughts, and hopelessness.

Living a life set apart from the word of God is disobedience. So, I helped Widows to cultivate a continual awareness of the presence of God that exists every day in their lives. Have you ever wanted to ask Jesus Christ to save, deliver, and heal you? Our teachings on healing broken relationships will show you the way. Bad choices will destroy the future of the widow. Let this book inspire you to do the right things and get the right results. Every widow should have inner peace which is found in Jesus Christ.

The world is working hard to achieve peace. But without Jesus, the Prince of Peace, we will never get it. World leaders recently held a global peace forum in Geneva Switzerland. Many international leaders tried to tackle global security and terrorism, which stood out as some of the most sophisticated and challenging issues to handle. War is a human-imposed disaster aimed at maximizing mass destruction through violent actions in order to achieve a political agenda.

On February 24th, 2022, Russia invaded Ukraine. The world was in chaos. This sudden invasion reminded me of how one day the Kiambogo village was surrounded by dangerous bush fire that was burning out from Eburu Forest. I thanked God that in this very painful experience in our lives I found His peace in our midst.

Thanks to God, we were safe from danger amid fierce flames of fire that were running first toward us and our houses. Three people were burnt to death as one man among them escaped miraculously from the flames. The villagers were amazed to see these survivors; they showed us a clear picture of what it means to be saved by God from danger. One of the survivors gained his conscious after three hours of being unconscious. He shared his powerful story of how the hand of God saved him from the danger of the fire.

I'm sharing my real-life stories to encourage all those widows and others who could be suffering like the people of Ukraine have. I want them to know that there is a God who can help you overcome any severe conditions, dangers, temptations, or oppositions, all of which could lead to death. In my life after overcoming very strong temptations, I became one of the most sought-after preachers and motivational speakers in the region. I've encouraged both believers and non-believers. I encourage people to seek God's wisdom and grace. I want to inspire you to resolutely trust in God and embrace every opportunity that He has provided for people.

In this book, you will learn how God can turn your life's problems to become fruitful experiences of His love. As you read, you will discover God's divine surprises, including peace, compassion, freedom, and salvation. As I wrote this book, I thought about how happy I am that God is guiding us and helping our Kenya defense forces to guard us from terrorists and other enemies.

Only if you repent and believe in Jesus will you receive eternal life. Otherwise, you will perish in Hell. My message to the widows and the world is simple: "repent or perish in Hell." Jesus is coming to separate the wheat from the chaff. He will gather the wheat in His barn, but He will burn up the chaff with unquenchable fire (Luke 3:17). I'm ready to go into the world with my hard-hitting messages of repentance. Repent, my friend, or else perish in Hell.

What is Hell? Probably the most familiar picture of Hell is that of torment and everlasting fire. Jesus himself spoke of hell fire. He described Hell as a place – "where the fire never goes out." The fire is never quenched. We read about the poor Lazarus in the Bible. "He was in torment and cried out in agony in the fire" *(Luke 16:23-24).* The fires of Hell were never really meant for human beings but rather for the Devil and his demons.

Hell means pain and punishment. It means total ruin. Thank God that I escaped from Hell. Before I was born again, I was sinking deeper and deeper into sin and its consequences. God's wrath was upon me. I was in Hell on earth. Hell sounds so horrible that people in the world insist that God would never send anyone to such a place; that God would never bring such punishment on anyone. However, the wages of sin are a fire that torments and consumes forever. Hell is the place where sinners get what they have chosen: eternal separation with God. Godlessness is worthlessness and hopelessness. Hell is hideous.

If God had not sent Jesus Christ to save me from sins, I would not have the possibility of escaping from Hell. I could have been doomed forever, but now I thank God that I escaped Hell. I was called by God to let you know the truth about Hell so that you can avoid it. Hell is a place for losers while Heaven is a place for winners. Are you still squandering opportunities and making excuses? Examine yourself in the light of the word of God. If you know that you are a loser, you need to change before it's too late. Admit to God that you are a sinner and repent by asking Jesus to forgive you. This could make you escape from an eternal death in Hell!

Our peace is being defended on the battlefield in Somalia by our selfless defense forces. So, I want you to find the way of peace in your hurting soul. In my lifetime, I will never forget the day I was born again and the day I was baptized in the Holy Ghost. When God gave me a vision of reaching the unreached and giving hope to the hopeless. When I started preaching in the village about salvation and healing.

I have seen widows and sinners repenting their sins after they discover the way of salvation. and. I've preached messages on repentance to widows, like John the Baptist, who looked wild and weird and spoke words that were fierce and jarring. "You bunch of snakes," he said to a crowd. "Who told you that you could escape God's wrath?" In my messages, I want people to undergo a complete turnaround. To change from the wrong direction. I want sinners to repent and accept Jesus Christ as their personal savior in order to escape the wrath of God. I want many people to escape from Hell. You had better change, or you will get the axe. Do you want to be thrown into the fire in the deepest depths of Hell?

Jesus has prepared me to warn you of the coming judgment you'll face if you don't repent of your sins. Will you? I have helped many people to come out of big problems, and they have changed their evil behaviors. I want you to experience change as well. God has sent me into the world to prevent people from going Hell.

What is the world coming to? people are wondering. The Russia/Ukraine war has continued without any cease agreement in sight. Russian forces are conducting "storming operations" in the Ukraine towns and cities. They don't want to obey orders from the United Nations to stop the operations. Many big buildings and big plants are reduced to ashes. The invaders are using air support weapons to strike. The reports around the world are telling us that cities, towns, buildings, and the entire critical infrastructure of Ukraine have been destroyed.

The whole world is wondering: Will the Russians stop their devastating artillery and rocket attacks? Ever since the invasion started in February 2022, civilians have died and others have been severely injured. In the world, there are strict orders to the Russians to categorically avoid attacks or strikes to civilians and infrastructure. Civilians are fleeing from death in Ukraine, and they are going to become hopeless refugees in the neighboring nations.

Speaking on behalf of their nation, the Ukraine soldiers said, "We shall defend our land and we shall fight. We will definitely defend our people and stand for them until the end. If we are to die, let's die for them." When the battle heated up, the Ukrainian military had no option but to begin a counteroffensive attack against their enemies.

This story is telling us that the word of God must come to pass...that before Jesus comes, nations will be rising against each other. The Bible states when you will be saying, "Peace and safety, then suddenly destruction comes." Are you struggling to fit into the comfort of this modern world? We are praying for Ukraine and praying for you to repent before it is too late.

Pray for those who are suffering in the battlefield because they need the hands of God. In Africa, we are ministering to those who are bound by the Devil in illicit brews, drug addiction, poverty, sex abuse, and violence. I am in a rehabilitation business. Our main objective is to take victims to a new level of victory where all of them would be 100 percent whole in spirit, soul, and body. "For I will restore you and heal your wounds, says the Lord" *(Jeremiah 30:17)*.

What a miserable life I lived in the Kiambogo village when I used to be high on drugs every day. I couldn't sleep. The hours would pass slowly during the night. I would see the first sun beam in the morning outside. I'd hear the birds singing while the day brightened. That was the state of my life before Jesus saved me from death. Jesus satisfied my inner being. I started helping victims to be delivered from stress and depression.

In my outreach programs, I've offered endless psychological and spiritual counseling. I've helped victims on how to escape from bondages, addictions, crimes, and bad situations and circumstances. The key to handling everyday stress in our lives is only found in the person called Jesus Christ. I'm telling young people that the way to handle stress-related problems is to repent of your sins and give your life to Jesus Christ. I'm introducing them to the digital world by assisting them on how to network through the Internet and social media so that they can earn money. I teach computer skills and how to make money on the Internet.

If you were to die with your evil behaviors, where would you spend eternity? Wouldn't it be the greatest disaster for you to die and end up in Hell? Don't be like the rich man in Luke 16:19-26 who died and woke up in Hell crying, "I'm tormented in this flame!" This book is a wake up call to troubled people whom the author is beseeching to repent and turn their lives around before it's too late. Call JESUS to deliver you from your evil behaviors before you die and go to Hell like the rich man. "How shall we escape if we neglect so great a salvation?" *(Hebrews 2:3).*

My programs are based to help eradicate hopelessness poverty, joblessness, idleness, alcoholism, sexual immorality, and HIV/AIDS transmissions. I would ask widows to kindly choose life and escape from hopelessness.

CHAPTER ELEVEN

LIVING BY FAITH.

VERONICA WAS A NAME given to my mother when she embraced religion as a Roman Catholic Christian. She was a committed follower of Christianity. One year after my brother, Dominic, died, she received the gospel, which was preached to her by members of our church, "Gospel Messenger's Church." She accepted Jesus Christ as her personal savior and joined our church. My father died in 1984 so my mother knew that as a widow she was to trust in God to provide for her needs.

As a committed believer, my mother was struggling to know the will of God in her life. She used to attend all meetings, Sunday services, and mid-week fellowships of believers. She loved the "keshas," the overnight vigils meetings held once in a month in Kiambogo village church. She was always led by the spirit and the word of God, which she obeyed in her Christian life. She confessed that she would keep her faith and conscience. She focused on doing the will of God. She trusted God to supply all her needs and she was always the first to give for missions and projects.

In September 2015, my mother's heart condition was worsening. She was taken to St. Mary's Hospital in Gilgil. After a few months, the shadow of death was hovering over her, and she stopped breathing. She died peacefully. We then started arranging for her burial. Many people, including family members, relatives, friends, believers, and pastors, attended her burial ceremony.

The Bible encourages us, "Precious in the sight of the Lord is the death of His saints" *(Psalms 116:15)*. My mum was a precious saint in our church. Although she left us suddenly, her prayers remained working for her children, grandchildren, and in the church. From the day she accepted Jesus Christ, she lived a better life with members of the church and her neighbors. In the village, she was a very successful farmer who kept livestock for her livelihood.

My mum lived in the Kiambogo village until she met her death. The Kiambogo village is about 45 kilometers from Nakuru Town and 35 kilometers from Gilgil Town. It is surrounded by the Eburu Forest from the east, home of the famous Bongo and many kinds of wild animals. Often, in the village at night, you could hear herds of buffalos from the Eburu Forest invading our crops. That's why the village was called "Kiambogo," which means, a "village of many buffalos." In the village, you could quickly note an acute water shortage during the dry seasons. Dams and rivers would be dry due to the prolonged drought. Women and girls would be forced to walk long distances in search of this commodity.

Many times, my mother used to retreat in prayer in what she called a "prayer season." She felt the Holy Spirit urging her to pray for her family and her church. She used to wake up very early, leaving her bed unmade, dishes unwashed, livestock unfed, and her garden unattended as she waited upon the Lord in prayer. She was an intercessor. When I visited her, she would tell me that I am in a prayer mood. I could hear her praying and mentioning all her children, grandchildren, and the church members by their names.

Writing my mother's story was not easy because members of the family are still agonizing for her loss. She brought us up for more than 66 years, helping us to survive in this hurting world. Mama, as we called her in our family, was a pillar to us, her children. She was very understanding, caring, loving, and compassionate; everything we could ask for in her. When she knelt down to pray, her prayers worked miracles in our lives. You could hear her praying and mentioning all the ministers of the gospel. She also prayed for other churches. She prayed for me and my ministry.

I was my mum's pastor and her mentor. She told God to sanctify me wholly and preserve me blameless until the coming of Jesus Christ. Sometimes, when preaching on a Sunday service, she would shout, "That's true! Say it all!" She advised me to preach messages that would build and add value to the souls of the congregation. She stood very firm in her spiritual convictions. She told her testimony without fear. She encouraged me to start a church ministry in her village. Whenever the church stood up to praise and worship, she would go forward in the pulpit to join the praise and worship team. She believed that she was called to praise the Lord.

The whole congregation admired my mum's unique dancing style. She meant business in the service to God. She encouraged her in-laws and grandchildren and always stood with them in prayer during challenging times. She encouraged believers with her moving testimonies. She endured and brought us up even when our dad died in 1984. My sister died in the year 2000 and my brother in 2003. Despite all this, she remained strong in her faith until the last minute.

Many believers, relatives, family members, friends, and neighbors came to celebrate the life of a precious saint. A life well lived. During my mum's burial, speeches, eulogy, and tributes were read by family members, grandchildren, and believers. Her burial was led by Bishop Tinkoi from Ngong, Nairobi. He read from the book of John 14:3. "And when I go and prepare a place for you, I will come again and will take you to myself; that where I am you may also be." The Bishop gave many life illustrations to describe the beautiful life beyond the grave. He knew my mum. To us, the family members, this was a very important day in our lives. The text had special significance to us and had a great revelation to us.

Before the burial, we had spent the whole night with spiritual leaders discussing the right person to lead the burial service. Every spiritual leader remembered how my mum used to give them gifts, prepare food for them, and make beds for them as guests. Her house was small, but she made sure that her guests were comfortable. We felt blessed when the Bishop spoke about my mother because he had visited her a few days before her death. He told the mourners that my mother had said to him that her house was ready in Heaven and that she was waiting for her day.

When the Bishop ended the sermon, he called us as a family to the front for prayers and encouragement. It was not easy for us, but God helped us to endure it with our children. We remained silent as the anointing from the Bishop flowed in our souls as he prayed for us. After the prayers, the Bishop led us to the grave where we laid the body of the precious saint who was my mother. The Bishop helped us to bury her with great peace and celebration. We gave our mother a wonderful send-off. We thanked our friends and our family members as they left the burial site with joyful faces.

Our family was comforted by the word of God: "Yea, though I walk through the valley of the shadow of death, I will fear no evil, for you are with me. Your rod and your staff, they comfort me" (*Psalms 23:4*). I am comforted to know that Jesus does not make mistakes. He knows all my needs, troubles, and sorrows. He knows my name, and he calls me by it. Jesus knew me from my mother's womb. He has known me from my childhood to now. He never mistakes me for anyone else. Jesus knows me well.

DO NOT WEEP

My mother always blessed and wished all her children well. She taught us endless and priceless values. Through her real daily example of living, she taught us how to love, share, care, and forgive; and more importantly, how to treat everybody well. She was our family's role model. She encouraged us her children to emulate Jesus Christ and keep our faith to the end.

I'm sure everyone who called my mother "cucu," grandmother, has memories concerning her. I know they have good memories; something they will always love to cherish. It was very often that they visited her and experienced the love of the old woman who was very special to them. She guided them as they called her "cucu." No matter how many times they felt messed up, her heart was always opened for them. She taught the boys how to behave like men and the girls how to act like women. She wanted all her grandchildren to do their best in their studies.

All children were taught to endure life and live without complaining. They were taught how to overcome the youthful lusts by believing in Jesus Christ. This kind of "cucu," one who loved them unconditionally and without discrimination, is very hard to find. My mother may not have approved of everything they did, but she appreciated them all without judgment.

Whenever they needed my mother, she was always there for them. She could listen, comfort, and encourage them. She lived a very simple life with her livestock. It did not take much to make her happy. A glass of milk, a piece of roasted meat, a phone call, a small gift, a visit, or a task well done is all you needed to put a smile on her face. Money can be squandered and property ruined, but what you inherited from your "cucu" cannot be damaged, destroyed, or lost. It is permanent, and it keeps her from becoming just a pleasant memory; it makes her alive in your lives forever.

To all who called my mother "maitu," you lost a special person in your lives. "Maitu" means great-grandmother. I know you always felt loved, wanted, and special. She made your childhood very special; some of the best memories you have of her. It did not matter what she was doing; she would have quality time with you. Your "maitu" played with you, chatted with you all night, and joked with you. She was always loving, compassionate, determined, and caring. I'm sure that you were touched by her love. You always felt proud to be with her.

Remember the songs and chorus. She sang for you as you waited for supper or lunch. How she prayed for you, asking God to enable you to perceive the truth so that you may be granted wisdom in your schooling and that you may be able to differentiate fact from fiction. She asked you to love God and obey His voice in your lives. She told you that one day she would go to Heaven.

My mother was relatively plump, a kind of woman who was considerably generous to the neighbors and relatives. She had a special gift of hospitality. She was very kind to all. Even though our resources were uncertain, Mother could always spare a cup of tea or a plate of food for any unexpected visitor. Mother was eloquent in her speeches, and she was always praying for her neighbors and friends. Through prayers, she believed everything is possible. With prayers, no burden could not be lifted, no storm could not be calmed, no sorrow could not be erased, and nobody could not be saved.

Mother prayed for broken marriages to be restored. She called all the villagers to come and drink the waters of life, but they ignored it. However, she kept her belief; there had never been a day in her life when she did not mention sinners to be saved. With her prayers, she attacked the kingdom of darkness as she pulled down the strongholds. Mother had indeed rested from her labors, trials, and tribulations in this hurting world. She is now in Heaven, where she wished to be free from death, pain, and sorrow.

Mum walked in her 86 years of a long journey of life with passion and determination to be like Christ. Mum was living by faith and went to be with the Lord on 21//9/2015. Today, I choose to remember my mother's life, strength, passion, wisdom, and golden heart. Although she was a widow she was. our pillar in life, and after her death, our heroine! She will be greatly missed by her children, friends, relatives, neighbors, ministers and members of Gospel Messengers Church.

Some people will never forget the good works of this departed saint. Mother is one of the founders of our ministry. Rest in peace. Fare thee well mum. I would encourage all widows to live by faith like my mum.

CHAPTER TWELVE

LIFE'S GREATEST DISASTER

THE FIRST ATOMIC BOMB in human history suddenly exploded over the Japanese town of Hiroshima, resulting in mass deaths and extensive damage that terrified mankind. Kenyans will never forget the 7/8/98 bomb blast in Nairobi, which left many dead and many others helpless with serious injuries. In September 2001, America was suddenly attacked by terrorists who hijacked airplanes and crashed them into the World Trade Center, causing an explosion of fire that left thousands dead and others severely wounded. The whole world lamented about this awful act of terror that caused fear to many people in America.

In the world today, there is a growing fear of what we call mass destruction by nuclear weapons. The whole world is still talking about these awful tragedies, which are caused by terrorists. Yet, the world fails to consider the horrifying fire and brimstone that is about to be revealed when the world comes to an end.

My friend, death is inevitable to all creations. So, when it eventually knocks at your door, where will you spend eternity? "I'm tormented in this flame." That was the agonized cry of one who had died and was buried before awakening in the eternal world of the damned. I want you to focus on the second death, which will be tormenting some of us. Even after reading the story of this man, you might still convince yourself that the second death and your reckoning with God is still a long way off.

In the story of the rich man and the poor man, Lazarus, the situation after death is clearly described. The rich man lived in sin, and after death he went straight to Hell. In Hell, he lifted up his eyes as he suffered pain, anguish, and torment. Poor Lazarus was righteous before God, so after his death, his spirit went to Abraham's bosom, where he would rest in paradise. But the rich man cried to God, "Have mercy on me and send Lazarus here so that he may dip the tip of his finger in water and cool my tongue! I'm tormented in this flame!" *(Luke 16:20-24)*.

My friend, you had better take note of this calamity and repent of your sins, lest you end up in the lake of fire like the rich man. I am persuaded to imagine that this might be the last warning you will receive from the Almighty God before He summons you into his presence. I pass to you God's warning: "Repent or perish in Hell."

"The fearful and unbelieving, whore mongers, sorcerers, idolaters, and all liars shall have their part in the lake which burns with fire and brimstone, which is the second death" *(Rev. 21:8)*. You might be living in sin like the rich man. You could be enjoying the pleasures of sin but soon end up crying in Hell with the rich man forever. What is the use of gaining the whole world and losing eternal life? Ask yourself that. "Treasures of the wickedness profit nothing, but righteousness delivers from death" *(Proverbs 10:2)*.

The story of the rich man stirs my heart and constrains me to be more diligent in persuading men to repent. Don't be like the rich man who fooled himself by trying to seek salvation when he was surrounded by eternal fire. It was too late for him. Millions are dying today not knowing what the future holds for them. The time for your salvation is now. "And it is appointed unto men to die once, but after this is the judgment" *(Heb. 9:27)*. Everything that you do is recorded in the books of God in Heaven and will be revealed to you openly on the Day of Judgment (Rev. 20:12-14). And whosoever is not found written in the Book of Life will be cast into the lake of fire (Rev. 20:18).

DO NOT WEEP

Why should you fear the second death when Jesus has shown you a clear way of escaping that fire and brimstone? If fear grips your heart at this time, it is probably because you know deep within your soul that you have never honestly opened up your sinful life to Jesus Christ, who is ready to cleanse you with His blood. So, will you call on the merciful savior right now?

The Bible has given you a chance to choose now where you will spend eternity. Remember that Jesus Christ is coming soon with your reward, which will be given according to your deeds. "He who is unjust, let him be unjust still. He who is filthy, let him be filthy still. He who is holy, let him be holy still. And behold. I come quickly with my reward to give every man as his work shall be" *(Rev. 22:11-12).*

The Blood Of Jesus Christ, God's Son, Cleanseth Us From All Sin (1 John 1:7). Have you experienced this cleansing? Be honest. Have you ever tried to walk into the light of God's presence in obedience to His word? Have you refused to accept the Savior due to preference for sin and pleasures like the rich man? No wonder you will tremble before your creator at His judgment throne. Even if your religion has been hypocritical of the Savior, to meet Him face-to-face is a must.

There will be no foolish bravado and no cheering audience. Your little fear will become unspeakable terror when you find yourself face to face with the Holy God you have despised. How often has He spoken to your heart offering Himself as your savior and you refused to listen? You prefer the sin that He hates. I would prompt you to repent your sins and avoid Hell. Why are you shutting your heart against the Savior's appeal?

"Come unto me, all ye who labor (under the bondage of sin) and are heavily laden (under the guilt of sins), and I will give you rest" *(Matthew 11:28)*. Yes, He is appealing to you now. I prophesy to you now that when you least expect it you will suddenly be in God's presence. A glance of faith at the Calvary and marks on Jesus Christ's body will silence your every excuse. Your sins and refusal of accepting a free pardon at the cost of the Savior's blood will sink you into Hell. The end is near, and the Savior is pleading in what may be the last plea.

At this moment, there is still hope for you, but after this, the Suddenly Nuclear Destruction Cometh that Almighty God has warned us about in the Bible will come as a thief who strikes in the night when no one is expecting it. God has graciously given us a number of signs to make us prepared when it happens. The day of Christ's Second Coming will come, and the sudden destruction will occur when people will be saying, "peace and safety."

Notice that the focus of people's thoughts today is on peace and safety. Let us think about the many peace movements that are spreading all over the world in which countless millions of terrified people, who know nothing of the inward peace of God in their hearts, are crying out for safety from nuclear destructions. May I ask, "How can we expect to find peace and safety on Earth while nuclear weapons are already aimed and allocated on vast areas for the destruction of the world at a moment's notice?"

There is a growing fear in this world today for what we call mass destruction by nuclear weapons. Moreover, may I assure you that there is no promise in the scripture of a future time of peace and safety? Long ago the Bible revealed this scaring truth: "'There is no peace,' saith the Lord to the wicked" *(Isaiah 48:22)*. So, I honestly believe that there is no person or nation that will bring peace on Earth when God has already declared war on a wicked and crooked generation.

DO NOT WEEP

Our God, who lived in ancient history, is the same God who lives and reigns among the nations today. Therefore, do not be moved by the peace motions or false peace movements that are encircling the globe today, but rather be concerned that your godlessness and your immorality may provoke God to declare war on you directly. "Who will save you then?" The rise in false prophets will try hard to lure you into a false sense of security by promising you a glorious, peaceful, and prosperous life on Earth while the word of God says that this Earth will melt with fervent heat.

Let me assure you that there is not a single promise of life of peace to sinners, whether AIDS victims, drug addicts, or drunkards, in the Bible. I stand firm to be corrected. If someone can show me such a scripture proving otherwise, I would be glad to concede. The everlasting life of peace is for all those who are washed by the blood of Jesus Christ (Romans 5:1).

Suddenly Jesus Will Be Coming. My dear friend, we are entering a final chapter of human history. But to all those who have trusted Jesus Christ as their personal savior, they have confidence about their future, for the Bible promises them a glimpse of heavenly bliss and eternal blessings that surpass comprehension. A day is coming when the Lord will be coming to take us home because we are the chosen generation who will usher in the glorious coming of Jesus Christ. We are anxiously waiting for the trumpet of God, which will blast through the air as we prepare to meet our savior.

Some of the end-time prophesies are being fulfilled before us: wars, famines, earthquakes, and natural disasters, as well as the critical world financial crisis, which is affecting every nation on Earth. Millions are dying today due to incurable diseases, wars, and starvation. I would urge you to flee to Jesus and let him save your life today. To have a Christian life is very promising because you shall live in a new world forever; a life of joy and fulfillment.

The time for you to decide to trust in Jesus is now. What opportunity is there after this? To all those who do not believe in Jesus, life is not promising. The Bible says the wrath of God will be poured out onto the earth, and there will be an incredible bloodshed; horror and eternal death forever. Remember that the Heavens and the Earth shall pass away in flaming fire on the day of the Lord. And suddenly Christ will appear in the clouds. "In such an hour as ye think not the Son of Man cometh. For as the lightning cometh out of the east and shineth even unto the west, so shall also the coming of the Son of Man be" *(Matthew 24:17)*.

Let me tell you my story. I was deep asleep at home in the Kiambogo village. Suddenly, in the middle of the night, I was awakened by loud screams of village women. Upon opening the door, I saw red flames of fire in a cloudless sky. The whole village was red with brush fire coming fast towards our houses from Eburu Forest. I rushed to the scene. Unfortunately, three people who were helping to put out the fire were caught unawares by flames that came flying over them. You could see them struggling and shaking in pain as their roaring voices soon became muffed dying whispers then silence and death.

This is why I'm telling the world that God's judgment is coming to all sinners refusing to repent. Don't be like the rich man who after he refused to repent died and awoke in Hell, crying, "I'm tormented in this flame!" *(Luke 16.19.26)*. Run to JESUS, and you will discover that He is the only one to make your life better forever. Do Not Weep, escape from hell by repenting your sins before it's too late! Missing Heaven by refusing to repent your sins would be life's greatest disaster. The hour of this awful revelation is at hand. Surely it is time to seek the Lord. When you shall be saying peace and safety... "Suddenly destruction cometh" *(1 Thess. 5:3).*

About the Author

PETER. N. MUYA HAS worked with Full Gospel Church and Redeemed Gospel Church, before starting his own ministry, Gospel Messengers Church.

He was born in 1955 in Nyonjoro farm, Lanet, Nakuru County. He has a Bachelor's degree in ministry, an associate's degree in biblical studies and Counseling.

He is married to Mary Muya, and they have three children who are adults working in different parts of our country. He is the founder and the Bishop of Gospel Messengers Church in East Africa.

About Us

Gospel Messengers Church is a nonprofit dedicated to transforming lives in Kenya's most marginalized communities. Committed to eradicating female genital mutilation (FGM), poverty, and illiteracy, the organization builds schools, provides clean water through boreholes, and empowers communities through education and sustainable development.

By addressing social injustices and uplifting vulnerable populations, Gospel Messengers Church fosters hope and opportunity for the less fortunate.

You can Donate via M-Pesa Pay Bill no: 880100 a/c: 5146870014.

You can also use PayPal email: messengergospel13@gmail.com

THESE ARE OUR BANK DETAILS FOR INTERNATIONAL MONEY TRANSFERS.

Bank Name	NCBA BANK KENYA PLC
Branch Name	NAKURU
Branch Code	000 (for any branch)
Bank Full Address	P.O. BOX 44599–00100, NAIROBI – KENYA
Bank Account Name	GOSPEL MESSENGER CHURCH
Bank Code	07
Bank Account Number	5146870014
SWIFT /BIC Code	CBAFKENX